Complicated Lives

Dear Scott,

Thank you !!!!

Steve

8/3/2019

COMPLICATED LIVES

Free Blacks in Virginia, 1619–1865

SHERRI L. BURR

CAROLINA ACADEMIC PRESS

Durham, North Carolina

Copyright © 2019
Sherri L. Burr
All Rights Reserved

See catalog.loc.gov for
Library of Congress Cataloging-in-Publication Data.

ISBN 978-1-5310-1617-3
e-ISBN 978-1-5310-1618-0

Carolina Academic Press
700 Kent Street
Durham, North Carolina 27701
Telephone (919) 489-7486
Fax (919) 493-5668
www.cap-press.com

Printed in the United States of America

For the Hills and the Burrs

Rest in Peace, Dear Relatives
Your Stories Continue

Contents

viii * CONTENTS

Author's Note

The road to creating this book has been paved with serendipity.[1] Sorting through a bag of letters in 2013, I found one from my great-aunt Callie informing me she was on her way to Wyoming because my great-great-aunt Lillian had taken ill. I remembered meeting Lillian once, at the funeral of my grandmother Juanita when I was six. I recalled Lillian as someone with straight black hair who looked more Native American than black. Two weeks later, another letter from Aunt Callie informed me that Lillian had passed away. From the security of my New Mexico home in 2013, I wondered why an African-American woman had lived in Wyoming in the middle of the last century. Contemplating this question started a journey that led to Virginia and across the Atlantic.

To uncover material for another book, I traveled to North Dakota, South Dakota, Wyoming, and Montana. On a stop in Worland, Wyoming, I explained to a sales associate that a relative had once lived there, and questioned how I could find her home and grave. She pulled out a map, and circled the county clerk's office and cemetery. Twenty-minutes later with the address to Aunt Lillian's home in my purse, I knocked on the door of her last residence.

Through a screen door, I saw a portly Hispanic woman with a kind face sitting on a chair. I introduced myself as Lillian Fay Todd's niece, and she said, "Come on in."

Mrs. Lucy Vigil explained that she knew Lillian well and had purchased the house and its contents from Callie who had inherited them. "The antique furniture had been shipped from Chicago," she said proudly.

As we talked, it occurred to me that I had inadvertently stumbled upon a family history museum. I departed Worland with gifts of Aunt Lillian's silver and handcrafted kitchen linens, along with even more questions.

A few months later, as I flew from Albuquerque to Salt Lake City to give a speech at the 2013 National Federation of Press Women Conference, I listened to a seatmate extolling the virtues of the Mormon Family History Library. Planning to check out the library for fifteen minutes, I disembarked from public transportation a stop short of the one nearest the conference hotel. Three hours later as the library was closing and a light drizzle fell upon Salt Lake City, I had missed dinner but had not noticed as I walked to the hotel with copies of digitized census records.

The paperwork contained a 1920 census record linking Aunt Lillian and her husband Andrew Todd to Chicago, and an 1850 census record identifying her father, George W. Hill, as having been born free in Virginia in 1847.[2] He resided in the household of his grandfather, Gideon Hill. The census record was titled "Free Inhabitants of Virginia." All the blacks and mulattos were designated with a B or M. The whites were not marked. George had an M next to his name, while a B was marked next to Gideon's.

Prior to this discovery, I lacked knowledge that there were blacks born free in the South before the conclusion of the Civil War. Like many Americans, I assumed all Africans were brought to the South as slaves and their descendants remained so until 1865. Unearthing this information led me to question just how many Free Blacks, like my ancestors, resided in Virginia and the rest of the South during the colonial and antebellum periods. What were their lives like? What legal rules governed their activities?

Seeking answers to questions like these led to this book. In researching the lives of my ancestors at the Library of Virginia, I discovered the document releasing Gideon Hill from bondage as a two-year old on January 25, 1787. More research at the Jefferson

Library in Charlottesville and other archives led to un-related individuals who had paid for liberty, earned their freedom through meritorious deeds, or were released from bondage due to the largess of planters motivated by honor or love.

If freedom is the God-given right of all people, this book contains stories of people of African origin who were never enslaved, born free, or who obtained liberty through court proceedings, sheer will, industriousness and entrepreneurship. They lived in an unpredictable society that sought to systematically deprive them of liberty and other human rights. This history of Free Blacks[3] in Virginia reveals the human ability to persevere against adverse odds arising from the color of their skin, or their gender, or both.

Complicated Lives is written using narrative nonfiction techniques to make sometimes stale history accessible to the general public. For example, with court records and other documents of known events, I modernized ancient dialogue from actual facts to tell the story. So that the reading of this book is not disrupted by footnotes, the source material can be found in the notes at the end of the book.

Revisiting a time when blacks were early citizens and participants in the United States economy proves black lives mattered then, and now. To heal the psychic injuries that continue today, we must unveil the past and address its wounds. This book interweaves legal history with my journey of discovering what happened to those African Americans who were free before the Civil War and lived their lives in the shadows of a complicated world.

Sherri Burr
Albuquerque, New Mexico

Hill Family Tree

✳

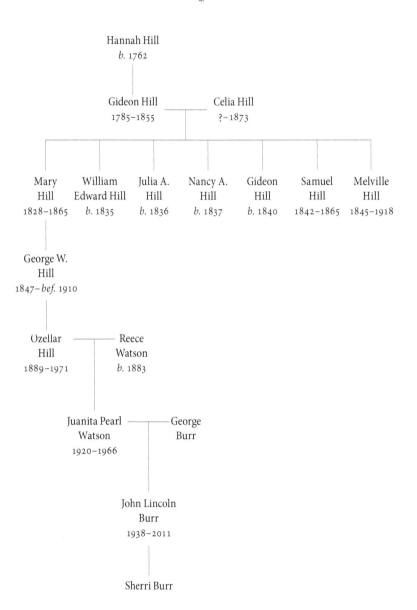

Hannah Hill
b. 1762

Gideon Hill ———— Celia Hill
1785–1855   ?–1873

Mary Hill	William Edward Hill	Julia A. Hill	Nancy A. Hill	Gideon Hill	Samuel Hill	Melville Hill
1828–1865	*b.* 1835	*b.* 1836	*b.* 1837	*b.* 1840	1842–1865	1845–1918

George W.
Hill
1847–*bef.* 1910

Ozellar ———— Reece
Hill   Watson
1889–1971   *b.* 1883

Juanita Pearl ———— George
Watson   Burr
1920–1966

John Lincoln
Burr
1938–2011

Sherri Burr

Benjamin & Suckey (Susannah) Crawley Family Tree

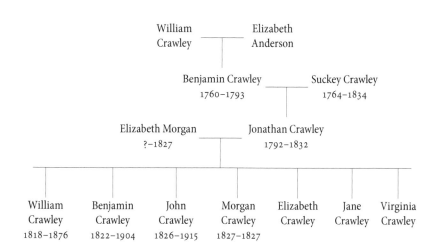

William Crawley ——— Elizabeth Anderson

Benjamin Crawley ——— Suckey Crawley
1760–1793   1764–1834

Elizabeth Morgan ——— Jonathan Crawley
?–1827   1792–1832

William Crawley 1818–1876 | Benjamin Crawley 1822–1904 | John Crawley 1826–1915 | Morgan Crawley 1827–1827 | Elizabeth Crawley | Jane Crawley | Virginia Crawley

Burr Family Tree

✳

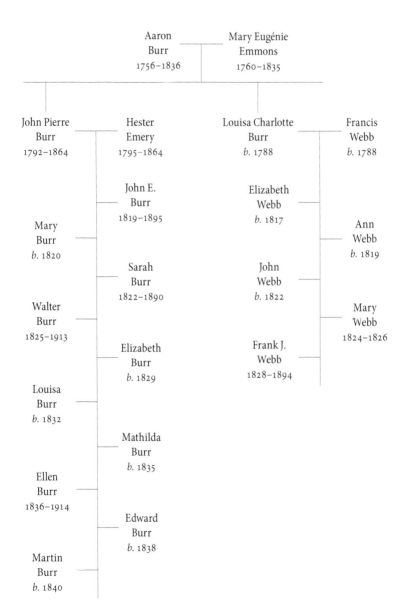

| Aaron Burr 1756–1836 | Mary Eugénie Emmons 1760–1835 |

John Pierre Burr 1792–1864 — **Hester Emery** 1795–1864

Louisa Charlotte Burr *b.* 1788 — **Francis Webb** *b.* 1788

Mary Burr *b.* 1820

John E. Burr 1819–1895

Elizabeth Webb *b.* 1817

Ann Webb *b.* 1819

Walter Burr 1825–1913

Sarah Burr 1822–1890

John Webb *b.* 1822

Louisa Burr *b.* 1832

Elizabeth Burr *b.* 1829

Frank J. Webb 1828–1894

Mary Webb 1824–1826

Ellen Burr 1836–1914

Mathilda Burr *b.* 1835

Martin Burr *b.* 1840

Edward Burr *b.* 1838

Thomas Jefferson & Sally Hemings Family Tree

✳

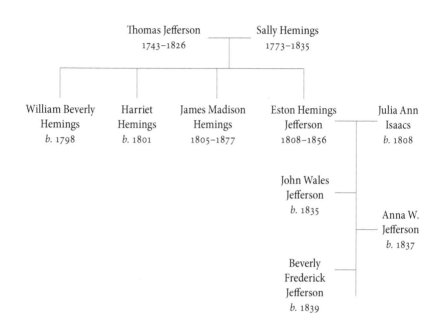

Thomas Jefferson
1743–1826

Sally Hemings
1773–1835

William Beverly
Hemings
b. 1798

Harriet
Hemings
b. 1801

James Madison
Hemings
1805–1877

Eston Hemings
Jefferson
1808–1856

Julia Ann
Isaacs
b. 1808

John Wales
Jefferson
b. 1835

Anna W.
Jefferson
b. 1837

Beverly
Frederick
Jefferson
b. 1839

Complicated Lives

✳

A Battle Over Freedom[1]

A n unlikely battle over freedom unfolded in 1653 on the grounds
of a Northampton County house[2] located on the Eastern Shore
between the Atlantic Ocean and Chesapeake Bay.

Captain Samuel Goldsmith, a commissioner (the early colonial
Virginia name for a judge), heard John Casor complain about the
actions of landowner Anthony Johnson. Two years before, Johnson
had received two hundred and fifty acres in Northampton County.[3]
Casor, who had been brought to Virginia from southern Africa
around 1640, sought his release from indentured servitude. This
early English labor system required a person to serve a term of years
without pay for a master before beginning an independent life.

In what arguably became a landmark set of proceedings, John
Casor said to Captain Goldsmith,[4] "I first served an indenture for
Mr. Sandys, another planter, before being brought to Mr. Johnson's
plantation. I served an additional seven years for Mr. Johnson. I
should have been released by now as my terms of service have exceeded the maximum of eight years permitted by law." Casor most
likely referred to George Sandys, the Virginia Colony's treasurer.[5]

"What say ye, Mr. Johnson? Where are Casor's indenture papers?"[6] Captain Goldsmith asked.

Most likely dressed in the typical homespun wear of the day, a dignified Johnson responded, "Captain, I have never seen indenture papers for Casor. I have the services of this Negro for his entire life."[7]

Captain Goldsmith probably looked skeptical. At the time, planters were expected to have indenture or other papers justifying the service of others.

"If I may, Captain, that is not true," Casor interjected. "Misters Robert and George Parker can confirm what I say."[8]

Eventually Captain Goldsmith asked Mr. Robert Parker and Mr. George Parker, "What say ye in this matter?"[9]

"I am Robert Parker, Captain. I confirm that this Negro, John Casor, was an indentured servant for Mr. Sandys on the other side of the bay. The indenture was then sold to Anthony Johnson. Casor has served his term for Johnson, and more."[10]

"Captain, if I may?" said the other brother. "I am George Parker. What Anthony Johnson has done to Casor is not fair. If he does not voluntarily release him, I ask you to order that Casor can recover Johnson's cows in compensation for services rendered which were not due."[11]

"Mr. Johnson, do you have a response to their demand?"[12] asked Goldsmith.

"May I have a moment to confer with my family?"[13] Johnson responded.

He discussed the matter quietly with his wife Mary,[14] two of his sons[15] and his son-in-law. "How will we till our fields without Casor? He's one of our strongest servants."[16]

"Husband," Mary whispered to Johnson, "You must let this Negro go. It will be the ruin of us if we have to give him all of our cows."[17]

"Father, I agree with Mother. You must let Casor go," said John Johnson, their eldest son, in a low voice. "We'll be shorthanded, but we'll make it work. Somehow, we'll find the extra hands."[18]

After his other son and son-in-law nodded their agreement, Anthony Johnson said, "Captain, my family and I have great fear over the loss of our cattle. I have been persuaded to set John Casor free."[19]

"So be it then," Captain Goldsmith declared. "John Casor, you are a free man."[20]

Casor and the Parker brothers probably shook hands as Anthony Johnson left with his head down. "It's not right,"[21] he said emphatically to his family. Casor was among the most diligent of Johnson's African and English servants tilling his 250 acres of land. Despite the assurances of his family, Johnson no doubt worried about harvesting his crops with one less worker.

*   *   *   *   *

Who was this Anthony Johnson who had proclaimed John Casor his servant for life, or a slave, from which there could be no release? Perhaps the most surprising fact: Anthony Johnson was born in Angola in the southwestern part of the African continent. Like John Casor, he was classified as a Negro in Virginia census records.[22] He had been brought to Jamestown almost two decades before Casor. At the time, no law designated all people of African origin as slaves.

Like many others from the same continent who lived in the early years of the Virginia colony, Johnson served a term of years as an indentured servant. Once released, he had slowly climbed his way to financial success through the acquisition of land. Now he had just let go of one of his heartiest servants in a conflict over who was entitled to freedom.

This first round of two proceedings between Casor and Johnson illustrated that being a Free Black in early colonial Virginia included the right to own all types of property, including servants. These individuals also had legal privileges to fight against those illegally proclaiming rights to their services.

Many twenty-first century Americans, like the author, possess DNA linking us to Bantu-speaking people of Angola in southern Africa. We owe a debt of gratitude to individuals like Casor and Johnson who survived the voyage, later called the Middle Passage, and servitude. They recreated themselves in a land far from their births. These gentlemen, their wives, and children were among the earliest Free Blacks living in Virginia.

ONE

✳

African Origins

Before he became Anthony Johnson, the Virginia plantation owner had been born as "Antonio"[1] in an Angolan village. In the early sixteenth century, Ndongo, the African kingdom of the Mbundu people,[2] had arisen from humble beginnings. Situated in the southwestern portion of the African continent, the men hunted antelope and other animals. The women cultivated crops and grew cassava, bananas, and additional vegetables and fruits. Ndongo occupied the highlands between the Cuanza (Kwanza) and Lucala (Lukala) Rivers.[3] The kingdom's people traded with their Kongo and Nziko neighbors. Sometimes they engaged in warfare, and captured their enemies, turning some into slaves and killing others. By the seventeenth century Ndongo became legendary because of Queen Ana Nzinga, who led many battles against invaders.

The Ndongo society dramatically changed after encounters with men who they later learned were from Portugal. Initially, Portuguese traded with Mbundu people and sought to introduce them to Catholicism. After the Mbundu rejected their proselytizing efforts, the Portuguese withdrew.

Around 1560, the Portuguese explorer Paulo Dias de Novais[4] brought Jesuit priests to Ndongo, and left one behind. Dias de

Novais later returned with an army and more priests. He launched war on Ndongo. The Ndongo King responded by ordering the Portuguese killed or expelled. When full war broke out, Kongo King Alvara sent armies to assist the Portuguese in wars against his people's ancient rivals. Once the Portuguese won, they expelled the Ndongo King from his capital of Kabasa, captured members of the royal family, and began exporting Ndongo captives to Brazil. Indeed, according to David Price, "The Portuguese and Imbangala attacks on Ndongo in 1618 and 1619 resulted in the enslavement of thousands; they were held in Luanda—now overcrowded by the penned-up humanity—until Portuguese or Spanish ships could haul them away."[5] All told, between 1500 and 1850, the Portuguese and Spanish shipped over 5 million people out of Angola. Anthony "Antonio" Johnson and John Casor were among them.

Not much is known about Johnson's and Casor's journeys from the area of their birth to Virginia.[6] We can only discern that they were either free individuals directly kidnapped by the Portuguese or Spaniards, or enslaved individuals through war-time captures who were traded by their countrymen to the Europeans. Both scenarios, and sometimes a blend of the two, resulted in many Africans being separated from their villages and kingdoms and forced to emigrate to foreign lands.

In a published slave narrative, Olaudah Equiano recalled being kidnapped from the kingdom of Benin.[7] He and his sister were left to mind their Eboe village home while the adults had left for work. Two men and a woman climbed their walls and seized them.[8] The kidnappers stopped their mouths, tied their hands, ran off with them into the nearest woods, and continued to carry them until they reached a small house where they paused for the night.[9] He and his sister were separated[10] and sold to different African masters. Equiano was eventually sold to Europeans and spent six or seven months on the ocean before coming to a sea coast.[11] A similar fate might have befallen either Johnson or Casor, or both.

Between 1451 and 1870, an estimated 20,000,000 to 25,000,000 Africans were ensnared into the slave trade. While there had been slavery in Africa and in other regions of the world for millennia, the volume and brutality of the Atlantic slave trade outstripped anything that had come before.[12] Thomas Jefferson, a slave owner and the third United States President, wrote about slavery as "a perpetual exercise of the most boisterous passions, the most unrelenting despotism."[13]

More than half of the African captives likely died in route to the coastline to board ships, or on the Atlantic voyage to a destination far from their homes. The number of individuals who actually arrived at their captors' intended destinations approximated ten million. Table 1-1, which contains data from E. Jefferson Murphy's *History of African Civilization*,[14] tells the story in rounded numbers:

TABLE 1-1. The Intended Destination of Slaves[15]

Area of Importation	Number of Slaves (1451–1870)	Percent
Portuguese Brazil	3,646,800	38.12%
British Caribbean	1,665,000	17.41%
French Caribbean	1,571,900	16.43%
Spanish America (Caribbean, Mexico, Central & South America)	1,552,000	16.22%
Dutch Caribbean	500,000	5.23%
British North America (U.S. and Canada)	427,300	4.5%
Danish Caribbean	28,000	0.3%
Old World (Europe, Atlantic islands)	175,000	1.83%
Total Number of Slaves	9,566,000	

Angolans, like Johnson and Casor, were among the 38.12% of all Africans headed toward either Portuguese Brazil or Spanish America to work in gold and silver mines or enormous sugar and tobacco plantations. At those destinations, the death rates were high

and the birthrates low.[16] Although modern minds associate British
North America, or what became the United States and Canada, as
the principle destination for slaves, less than five percent of African
captives actually ended up arriving in this area. Africans who were
shipped to British North America had lower death rates and higher
birth rates, and thus the numbers grew internally.[17]

Johnson and Casor had their intended voyage to Portuguese Brazil or Spanish America intercepted, similar to an offensive team's
quarterback throwing a pass intended for his team's running back
only to have the football picked off by the defensive team's corner-
back. For Anthony "Antonio" Johnson, his journey was redirected to
Virginia after he and fellow captives were kidnapped on the Atlantic
Ocean by men pirating a schooner called *The James*.

＊　＊　＊　＊　＊

How Antonio ended up on the High Seas is a mystery. Like many
living in a traditional Angolan kingdom, Antonio may have already
been an enslaved person who had been captured by another tribe
and subsequently traded to the Portuguese. In his book *The History of African Civilization*, Professor Murphy wrote that Africans
imported a wide variety of European goods (such as cloth, rings,
paper, shoes, and sugar)[18] in exchange for "[i]vory, pepper, gum,
skins, beeswax, ostrich feathers, and slaves."[19] The longer the Portuguese trade continued, Murphy added, "the more important the
slaves became in it" and eventually "European demand for African
Slaves far overshadowed demand for all other African goods."[20]

If not already a slave, Antonio may have been hunting game with
his father and siblings on what began as a normal day when he
was captured. He could have climbed a mopane tree to obtain a
good view and tell his elder where to look for game, only to have
descended into hands that threw a bag over his head.[21] In such a
scenario, he would have kicked and punched as he listened to his
father call his name from a distance, "Antonio, Antonio."

Perhaps he yelled back, only to have a hand cover his mouth and stifle his screams. As he was carried away, his father's voice probably sounded more desperate as it faded into the wind.

Antonio may have trembled with fear as the men whispered to each other in Portuguese. He probably knew this as the language of the pale ones, those much lighter in complexion than his Mbundu kinsmen. His father or another village elder may have taught him to both read and write Portuguese. Word may have long ago spread to Ndongo villages that these Portuguese were not priests, but *degredados*,[22] known for murdering and stealing in their own country. In *Angola under the Portuguese: The Myth and the Reality*, Gerald Bender argued that "the overwhelming majority of the Portuguese in Angola were exiled convicts, or *degredados*. In fact, *degredado*s constituted the vanguard of the forces which attempted to penetrate the hinterland during the first century of Angolan colonization."[23]

The Portuguese were also notorious for forcing their captives to march in chains to ships. Using weapons, *degredados* forced Angolans below deck and bound their feet and hands. No Angolans from any of the kingdoms are likely to have volunteered to leave their homes and families for this unknown fate. It is also possible that some brutality inflicted on captives by *degredados* may have been reported to villagers by escaped kinsmen who returned to tell what happened to them. Either way, one can imagine that Antonio trembled in the presence of *degredados*.

TWO

*

The Voyage

Awakening on a rocking ship, Antonio probably felt frightened
because the waves did not resemble the rivers his Mbundu people
used for fishing and where vessels voyaged smoothly. He no doubt
thought about his mother and siblings cultivating their fields, gathering eggs from chickens, or milking goats in the Ndongo village.

All the captives must have feared never seeing their families
again, and their family members probably experienced deep dread
for their spouses, siblings, and children who had not yet returned
from daily outings. In Olaudah Equiano's narrative,[1] for example,
he wrote of the grief that his mother and friends might have experienced when they had returned home to discover that he and his
sister were missing.

Based on recreated ships from the era,[2] the captives were held in
dark, damp quarters. Sheer terror probably led to uneven breath-
ing and their sweat permeating the space. Their hands were shack-
led and their feet bound by chains. Equiano wrote in his narrative
about the trepidation invoked by such sights and smells.[3]

On Antonio's original ship out of Angola, he was likely sur-
rounded by people who spoke his language. Other voices and dia-
lects may have belonged to his peoples' ancient enemies. On these

ships, the Ndongo, Kongo and Nziku captives had a common foe: the Portuguese.

The wretched journey had to entail moments permitting captives to eat, relieve themselves, and exercise. The Portuguese *degredados* probably took care to line their captives in a manner that led to maximum order as they shuffled from below deck toward the light shimmering off the Atlantic Ocean.

Occasionally permitted to breathe in the fresh ocean air, the captives must have wondered how long had they been at sea. With no land on the horizon, they no doubt found it difficult to judge how far away they had sailed from their homeland.

As nights blended into days on Antonio's journey, something changed on one of them. In the distance another vessel sped toward them.

Sudden panic must have invaded the atmosphere. *Degredados* probably shouted to each other in Portuguese, "Look at that ship coming toward us," or, "It travels fast. It looks hostile."

Antonio and the other captives who might have been above deck when the schooner was spotted were most likely immediately hustled below to the cargo bay. The Angolans undoubtedly placed their ears to the ship's wall to hear the fighting of metal hitting metal and death screams piercing the walls.

At some point the cargo hatched opened and different pale-skinned men descended. Antonio and his kinsmen rose and shuffled up the narrow stairs with the new arrivals. They probably saw several *degredados* with blood oozing from deep wounds, eyes wide open as if experiencing the shock of the sudden escape of their spirits to another dimension.[4]

The new men hustled Antonio and the others toward another vessel. Antonio perhaps understood the letters on the side of the ship, *J-a-m-e-s*,[5] as he most likely had learned the Portuguese alphabet. However, he probably did not know what the word meant.

After the captives were aboard, these paler men likely directed them toward their hatch so that Antonio and the others could descend their tapered stairs and have their chains refastened. The ship set sail. Antonio and the others had no idea where they were headed. Their hands probably shook and they fought tears. Some might have sobbed. They had been kidnapped a second time and probably lost all hope of ever seeing their families again.

* * * * *

Aboard the *James*, perhaps the captives scratched thin lines in the ship's wooden sides, or counted their fingers and toes multiple rounds, to mark their days at sea. The routine of occasionally being brought up deck to eat, breathe fresh air, walk, and relieve themselves likely continued. Perhaps the captain and deckhands began teaching the captives their language by gesturing to items and stating words in English. Holding up fingers could have been used to teach captives how to count in the new language.

The days no doubt passed slowly as Antonio and the others learned some of the language of the English and journeyed toward an unknown land. Numerous lines in the wall or counting rounds of fingers and toes later, the *James* docked on land. Antonio and the others were hustled above deck. They had left Angola in the warm, rainy season. It might have been raining in the new land as chills likely crept up Antonio's spine and that of others in the boat.

He was counted among the approximately 427,300 Africans who left Angola, or passed through Senegal's "Door of No Return"[6] and similar structures in other countries, to land in British North America.

THREE

*

Virginia

In 1621 the *James*, with Antonio on board, sailed into a tri-racial community containing indigenous peoples, English settlers, and kidnapped Africans who had begun arriving in late August 1619. This was a year before Mayflower Pilgrims landed on Plymouth Rock. The first English males had taken four months to cross a stormy ocean before disembarking from their ships the *Susan Constant*, *Discovery*, and *Godspeed*[1] in 1607. Most of these immigrants had bound themselves in servitude to the Virginia Company. In return for a one-way ocean passage and a share of the company's profits, they had committed to obey the leaders and work without wages.[2]

The England from which the settlers left had been governed for four years by King James I, who had inherited the country after Queen Elizabeth slipped into a coma and did not awake on March 24, 1603.[3] James Charles Stuart had been born on June 19, 1566, to Mary, Queen of Scotts, and her husband Lord Darnley in Edinburgh Palace.[4] As Elizabeth's second cousin, Mary Stuart was the heir to the throne of England until Elizabeth forced her to renounce her claim in favor of her son. He was crowned James VI of Scotland at the tender age of thirteen months.[5]

After becoming England's sovereign, James I had been labeled by some as "the wisest fool in Christendom." He, however, had proclaimed on a visit to Oxford, "If I were not a King, I would be a university man."[6] This division between how the English viewed the first Scotsman to ever govern them and how that educated Scotsman, who spoke and wrote multiple languages and who authored books, viewed himself, personified the reign of James I. Eventually, he not only lent his name to the James River, the *James* ship, and Jamestown in the New World, but also to the *King James Bible*. Meanwhile, he was demonized in England as a spendthrift and for his openly affectionate relationship with George Villiers, the Duke of Buckingham and Gentleman of the Bed Chamber.[7]

On the other side of the Atlantic, the colonists initially encountered and dined with the Kecoughtans, a tribe numbering fewer than a hundred, the Paspahegh, the Rappahannock, and the Appomattoc, in April 1607.[8] While the Paspahegh and the Rappahannock warmly welcomed the English, the Appomattoc met the colonists with warriors bearing bows, arrows, and swords.[9]

By the time the English engaged with these local tribes, one study later estimated that over 55 million indigenous peoples had lost their lives from contacts with other Europeans during the prior century.[10] The arrivals of such legendary explorers as Christopher Columbus in the Bahamas in 1492 and Hernán Cortés in Mexico in 1519 led to the loss of an estimated 90% of the indigenous peoples because of the diseases the Europeans brought with them, from which the indigenous peoples had no immunity.[11] Their rampant demise equally devastated the environment, which "may have contributed to a period of global cooling."[12]

The Powhatan tribe initially made friendly visits, fed, traded with, and welcomed the English.[13] After the death of his wife and daughter, John Rolfe courted and married Chief Powhatan's daughter, Pocahontas.

Conflict inevitably developed between the Powhatan Indians and the newcomers. They shared neither a language nor a culture to aid in communication. War ensued. Captain John Smith was twice captured and twice rescued by Pocahontas when she was a maiden. Unable to appropriately cultivate the land, starvation claimed English lives. As David Price noted in *Love and Hate in Jamestown*, "the winter of 1609–1610 became known as 'the Starving Time.'"[14] By March 1610, only sixty colonists remained out of five hundred in Jamestown.[15]

Leaving England permitted the settlers a chance to govern themselves. They did so by establishing a General Assembly, later named the House of Burgesses, in 1619. The colony slowly rebounded and had become self-sustaining when the *White Lion*, a 160-ton ship, navigated the James River in late August 1619, with "20 and odd" Africans on board. The *White Lion* led by Captain Jope had teamed up with a ship out of Jamestown, the *Treasurer* led by Daniel Elfrith or Elfirth, to attack the Portuguese ship *São João Bautista*.[16] The *São João Bautista* had left Angola with 350 Africans aboard, and was subdued with no shots fired. Both the *White Lion* and the *Treasurer* exchanged food for human cargo.[17]

Jope arrived on the *White Lion* with 20 Africans, and Elfrith followed a few days later with just over 30 Africans on the *Treasurer*. They sailed into Point Comfort (now Hampton), Virginia, a distance of about 32 miles from Jamestown. Captain Manuel Mendes de Acunha eventually sailed the *São João Bautista* into Veracruz, Mexico, with 147 Africans on board.[18] Of the initial 350 Angolans on board the *São João Bautista* when it departed the West African coastline, only about 197 had reached land on the other side of the Atlantic Ocean. Thus, fifty-six percent of the Africans were accounted for, and presumably the other forty-four percent perished during the voyage.

The Africans who arrived in Virginia were equally divided between men and women. However, they had arrived into a Virginia colony demographically lopsided with seven English men to one English woman.[19]

In suffocating August humidity, the Africans were put to work alongside English indentured servants to harvest tobacco by cutting down plants to be left overnight to sweat.[20] The House of Burgesses passed no laws or decrees declaring these first Africans to be slaves. Rather, these kidnapped African immigrants appeared to have been given the status of indentured servants, like their English counterparts, who were required to work for a term of years before securing rights to pursue independent lives. As Judge A. Leon Higginbotham wrote *In the Matter of Color*, "From 1619 to approximately 1660 there appears to have been no systematic effort in Virginia to define broadly the rights or non-rights of blacks."[21]

Indeed, as further evidence that the initial African immigrants were not treated as slaves, David Price wrote that Captain John Smith had "denounced Englishman Thomas Hunt for capturing twenty-seven natives in present-day Massachusetts in 1614 and selling their 'poore innocent soules' into Spanish slavery."[22] Another colonist, John Pory, had written about how "Hunt had most wickedly stole away" natives to sell into slavery.[23] If these men were condemning the enslavement of indigenous peoples, they were unlikely to be engaged in the slave trade themselves.

One of them had personal experience with enslavement. In 1602, John Smith had been captured in a battle in present-day Romania, auctioned, and sold into slavery on a Turkish farm.[24] Smith escaped by beating his master to death, putting on the man's clothes, and riding off on his horse.[25] Smith thus had good reason to condemn the inhumane activity.

* * * * *

When Antonio arrived in Jamestown on the *James* in 1621, two years had passed since the first Africans had been integrated into colonial society. His captain may have announced to the English, "These people are available to work as servants on your farms and plantations. You must pay for their transport to acquire the right to their servitude." Such a statement was consistent with how the labor of indentured servants was obtained.

English people probably gathered around and examined Antonio and his fellow captives. Men likely approached and gestured for them to open their mouths to examine their teeth to assess their

THREE. VIRGINIA ✳ 21

worthiness for helping on their land. Had Antonio been a slave in
Angola, such an examination might have been familiar. Were he
instead a kidnapped member of a royal family, then he could have
felt insulted and been reluctant to participate.

A ship captain or auctioneer probably announced in reference to
Antonio, "Sold to the Bennett plantation. Mr. Bennett, please settle
up with the sailors."[26] Since there are no records as to the transac-
tion by which Antonio became an indentured servant, we are left to
speculate as to what happened. In this instance, Bennett most likely
handed bags of tobacco, or something else of value, to the seamen
before walking toward Antonio and saying to him, "You're coming
with me," as he pointed to a small boat with oars.

As they maneuvered the south side of the James River toward
the Bennett plantation, Antonio probably considered his situation.
He had voyaged far from home, and likely wondered about ever
seeing his family again. Traveling in a strange boat with a stranger
or strangers, tears probably dripped down his young face.

If Bennett was a compassionate person, he empathized with the
plight of his young servant and said something like, "You'll be all
right. I know you're a long way from home. This must be scary. My
name is Mr. Bennett and we are rowing to my brother's plantation,
Warresquioake."[27] Given the language barrier between the English
colonist and his newly acquired indentured servant, such a conversation required further phonetic attempts, such as breaking out the
name of the plantation by syllables, "War-res-qui-oake."

Antonio likely slowly pronounced the word several times while
Bennet perhaps tried to explain that his brother's plantation was
located on the south side of the James River. He likely introduced
Antonio to the tobacco plant by removing some green leaves from
his pocket and handing them to Antonio, while gesturing for him
to smell them and feel their stickiness.

By 1619, tobacco had become the colony's most lucrative export
crop, despite the antithesis of King James I. The sovereign encouraged the colonists to plant vineyards and raise silkworms instead of
tobacco, but to no avail.[28]

Considering the plant was unfamiliar to Antonio, he likely sniffed, grimaced, and returned the foul smelling items. Bennett could have laughed and further explained that on his brother's plantation they grow vegetables and raise cattle. He then could have air-gestured to demonstrate a large animal. For Antonio, such a shape might have connoted a goat. As they continued their journey on the James River, any conversation suffered from inability of each to speak the other's native tongue.

✳ ✳ ✳ ✳ ✳

At Bennett's plantation, Antonio settled into the servants' quarters with approximately fifty people. Most were English, but probably some were Mbundu from Kabasa. The Africans had been captured by the Portuguese two years before in the intense battle for the capital of Ndongo and brought to Virginia by the *White Lion* ship.[29]

As Antonio got to know his fellow kinsmen with whom he could communicate in their common tongue, they probably explained how *degredados* had slaughtered their families and seized them. They were marched to the ocean and placed upon the *São João Bautista*. At the time, the Portuguese had been engaged in a war of expansion against the kingdom of Ndongo.[30]

On the Bennett plantation, Antonio could have been assigned to either work the tobacco fields or herd the cows in the pastures. Both activities required a learning curve since tobacco was not cultivated in Angola and the traditional people herded goats rather than cows. Antonio's kinsmen may have explained the similarities and differences between goats and cows. Goats are known to engage more with humans than cows who often stand straight and stare into the distance for seemingly hours on end. Antonio could have also been introduced to cow's milk, and perhaps he made favorable or unfavorable comparisons to goat's milk.

If assigned to herd cattle to pasture, Antonio probably did so at predawn for several months before one fateful Thursday evening when he returned to the servants' quarters at the Bennett Planta-

tion to find the other indentured servants with food he had never
seen before. The Powhatan Indians brought the items to the plantation earlier that day. In preparation for the Christian holiday of
Easter the following Sunday, the Bennetts had traded English tools
for Indian food.[31] Antonio probably took bites of bittersweet fruits
that both repelled and attracted him before bedding down for the
evening in the servants' log cabins.

* * * * *

At daybreak on Good Friday, March 22, 1622,[32] Antonio headed
to the pasture to walk the cows. Suddenly, in the distance someone may have screamed, "Powhatans! Powhatans!," as other noises
sounded the alarm. The other indentured servants had likely told
Antonio that if he ever heard certain sounds, the plantation was
under attack.

Since the English tended to reserve the weapons for themselves,
Antonio and his kinsmen might have lacked a method of defense
other than to hide. Upon hearing shouting, Antonio probably ran
toward the tallest tree with the fullest branches. The one that most
resembled the Angolan mopane most likely provided comfort for
those forced to immigrate to this different world.

The Powhatans attacked with the axes, hoes and other metal
instruments they had obtained from the English the day before.[33]
Shots rang out and several Indians fell. Other Indians shot arrows,
which pierced English hearts. Antonio likely listened to the screams
of death, which needed no language interpretation.

* * * * *

As nightfall approached, he likely observed the stillness. The movement had ceased, and so had the moans. Should he climb down?
No, wait.

The moon brightened the grounds as he peered out from his
hiding place. No movement in the distance. Silence. Antonio likely
gingerly dismounted from the tree, glancing down with every step.
Once satisfied that no one waited below, he probably jumped to the

ground, and slowly approached the pasture. Many cows were dead. Some were missing.

Heading toward the servants' quarters, he might have seen bodies with blood escaping from every crevice. Some had dents in their heads where they had been felled with the traded English axes, whereas others had sliced-up chests or arrows piercing different body parts. Antonio probably resisted the urge to vomit, and made himself breathe to still the rate of his heart. He silently searched, slowly moving forward until eventually encountering Mbundu kinsmen perhaps hidden in other trees.

An exchange in their Bantu language could have brought the comfort of knowing they were not dealing with an enemy. As Antonio and his kinsmen snuck toward the servants' quarters, more death stung their nostrils and shocked their eyes. They likely decided to head back to their hiding places and wait until daybreak to assess the situation.

✳ ✳ ✳ ✳ ✳

The next morning they counted fifty-two dead and found two other men alive.[34] An English servant and Mr. Bennett were slightly wounded, and they likely had played dead to escape further injury from the Powhatan attackers. Mr. Bennett probably pleaded with Antonio and his kinsmen to listen to him as they tended to his injuries. "You can run away," he could have said, "and no one will look for you. But if you stay and help us rebuild, I will see that you obtain indenture papers so that eventually you will be completely free."

Antonio and his kinsmen likely looked at each other and considered the bargain before agreeing. They likely nodded their assent. This scenario of a bargain presents a plausible explanation of how Antonio obtained indenture papers and began his transformation from Antonio, the forced immigrant, to Anthony Johnson, the plantation owner.

His first task toward complete liberty: bury the dead.

✳ ✳ ✳ ✳ ✳

Later in 1622, a ship named the *Margrett and John* sailed into the Virginia colony with Mary, an Angolan woman, on board.[35] Bennett purchased the rights to her servitude for the Warresquioake plantation. When Antonio looked at her, something probably fluttered in his heart. For the first time since he had left his homeland, he may have felt happy to be exactly where he was.

His kinsmen probably liked Mary as well, but she preferred Antonio. Eventually, he asked her to become his wife and she accepted.

Mr. Bennett accommodated their arrangement by giving them separate servant quarters. The 1624 to 1625 colonial census listed twenty-three Africans, which included Antonio and Mary. Since their designation was as servants, they received the same class name as many English.[36] By 1625, Mary was the only woman living on the Bennett plantation. They named their first son Richard, probably to honor Mr. Bennett. As Antonio became more assimilated and comfortable in his new environs, he anglicized his name to Anthony and adopted the English surname of Johnson, which Mary also took.

County records created between 1632 and 1661 designated people of African descent as "servants," "negro servants," or simply "negroes," but never as "slaves."[37] This temporary servitude was different from slavery because, as one historian opined, "The loss of liberty to the servant was temporary; the bondage of the slave was perpetual."[38] As a new colony, the Virginia settlers slowly developed their own law and custom toward all arrivals, including Anthony and Mary Johnson.

FOUR

＊

Property

A nthony Johnson had lived in Virginia for two years, and Mary Johnson for a year, when in 1623 the House of Burgesses adopted a statute requiring that "Every freeman shall fence a quarter of an acre of land to make a garden for planting vines and herbs and mulberry trees."[1] "Freeman" was the word initially used to reference those who had completed indentured servitude.[2] This policy ensured that the colony could feed and economically sustain itself.

The indentured servitude system encouraged the English to leave their homes and settle in the new mysterious continent. The richer English paid the passage of the poorer ones. In return, the poor serviced the farms or plantations of the rich for a term of years, depending on the contract. The land patent system permitted the rich to grow their holdings through headrights.

On July 22, 1634, the Royal Government of Virginia started issuing patents for headrights.[3] The Virginia Company had defined headrights as "[t]he right to receive fifty acres per person, or per head" to encourage immigration into the colony.[4] Further, "any person who settled in Virginia or paid for the transportation expenses of another person who settled in Virginia should be entitled to receive fifty acres of land for each immigrant."[5] "Headrights" were one of three ways that land was acquired in colonial Virginia. The other two methods were (1) for special services and (2) for consideration, such as the payment of one pound of tobacco per year.[6]

From 1607 to 1643, servants without contracts became free after serving two to eight years.[7] After 1643, the terms were fixed between four and seven years, depending on the youthfulness of the servant.[8]

Farmers claimed headrights on each member of their families, including children and servants.[9] Children brought economic value to family units because the more births, the more land their parents received. Additionally, the more individuals imported to work their land, the more acres farmers acquired to call their own. Consequently, the largest estates were built through births and by importing people from England, Africa, or the West Indies to work the land.[10]

In 1635, Anthony and Mary Johnson went to live on the plantation of John Upton, who petitioned for more land after purchasing their headrights, or the right to their servitude, probably from Bennett. Upton must have assured them that after four years of service they would finally receive their complete liberty. In the same year the Johnsons moved to the Upton plantation, Virginia began permitting Free Blacks to acquire headrights and land patents.[11]

By 1639, Anthony and Mary had started their own farm. Since Angolans practiced shifting cultivation and the rotation of different crops, the Johnsons were well equipped[12] to begin working for themselves. They had been born into a skilled people who were known for turning metals, including iron and copper, into pottery, weaving mats and articles of clothing from raffina tissues and palm cloth, and domesticating animals, including pigs, sheep, and chickens.[13] They had also acquired additional knowledge about the particular nature of the Virginia farmland from their years as indentured servants.

In 1639, the Virginia House of Burgesses began a racialist swerve by enacting laws that distinguished between the rights of the English and those of African immigrants. Virginia legislation Act X stated, "All persons except Negroes are to be provided with arms and ammunition or be fined at the pleasure of the governor and council."[14] However, T.H. Breen and Stephen Innes postulated[15] that the law did "not prohibit a black master such as Anthony Johnson from possessing a firearm, nor for that matter, [did] it order all blacks regardless of their status to surrender their weapons to the state. And finally the law [did] not make it illegal for blacks to engage in offensive or defensive warfare." This is a fair interpretation since the law addressed distributing weapons from the government, as opposed to removing weapons from individuals. Thus, presumably Free Blacks could keep the weapons they had already acquired and purchase weapons privately. In 1723, Virginia clarified that a Free Black or mulatto who was a housekeeper could keep one gun, and that all Negroes, mulattos, or Indians, bond or free, and living at any frontier plantation were permitted to keep and use guns.[16]

While the motivation behind the 1639 law was not stated, fear could have been the inspiration. Higginbotham discussed the rising panic associated with potential alliances among white indentured servants, Indians, and blacks.[17] He wrote that in 1640, "the General Virginia Court decided the *Emanuel* case, which involved a black who participated in a conspiracy to escape." Along with six white servants, he stole "the skiff of Pierce and corn, powder, and shot guns, which said persons sailed down the Elizabeth river" before being captured and convicted.[18] All the whites received added years to their terms of servitude, and some were both whipped and branded. The black man, Emmanuel, however, "was whipped, branded with an 'R' on his cheek, and required to wear shackles for one year."[19] Because Emmanuel did not receive additions to his original term of service, Higginbotham speculates that he may have already been "a servant for life, making a sentence of extra years of service an empty gesture."[20]

In another instance, a Dutchman, Scotsman, and black man, all of whom were indentured servants, ran away together. When apprehended, the Dutchman and Scotsman had a year added to their servitude for their masters plus an additional three years of service to the colony. John Punch, the black man, was sentenced "to serve his master or his assigns for the time of his natural Life here and elsewhere" in the case of *In re Negro John Punch.*[21] This imposition of a lifetime of servitude for the person of African descent was not based on any previous statute or judicial proceeding,[22] but rather indicates the beginnings of differentiation between punishments imposed on blacks and whites who committed the same act. In this case, they all ran away from their indentured servitudes. Punch's life was not in vain, for his genetic legacy would lead directly to the first African American President of the United States, Barack Obama, in 2009.[23]

Just as the Virginia colonial government began limiting its distribution of weapons based on race, and Virginia judges began imposing different sentences for whites and blacks who committed the same illegal acts, Anthony and Mary Johnson had commenced building their fortune based on land and farming. In 1648, James Berry, Edward Douglas, and John Winbery all sold cows to Anthony Johnson. Berry sold him a calf, Douglas, a yearling heifer, and Winbery a red cow.[24]

In 1651, the colony assigned Anthony Johnson two hundred fifty acres of land on Pungoteague Creek, an inlet on the western side of Northampton County.[25] He had paid for the passage of several servants, some of whom were English.[26] The five names listed on his petition were Thomas Bembrose, Peter Bughby, Anthony Crips, John Gesorroro, and Richard Johnson.[27] Anthony and Mary's son, John Johnson, was granted 550 acres in 1652 after he paid the cost of eleven servants to enter the colony. Similarly in 1654, a Richard Johnson, perhaps the same Richard Johnson who had been Anthony Johnson's servant, received 100 acres in 1654 for having paid the cost of transporting two servants.[28] The colony accorded another Free Black, Benjamin Doll of Surry County, 300 acres in 1656 for transporting six servants.[29]

Six years after Johnson imported English males, the House of Burgesses passed a law prohibiting Negroes from owning English indentured servants but they could continue to own Negroes. Nonetheless, historian Luther Porter Jackson estimated that at least another four Free Blacks received 1,200 acres of land under the headrights system during the 1650s decade.[30] After 1660, Jackson uncovered further land grants to blacks under the headrights system, but he did not specify the race of the servants whose transportation cost payments permitted the grants.

In 1652, fire engulfed the Johnsons' land and destroyed their crops. With no way to pay their taxes, they successfully petitioned the court for relief for themselves and their two daughters.[31] This event occurred during a time when taxes were assessed on people and not on land or livestock.[32] The House of Burgesses had declared all Negro men and women, and all other men from ages sixteen to sixty, to be tithable in 1644,[33] and repeated that requirement for Negro women in 1668.[34] Act VII (1668) provided, "Negro women though permitted to enjoy their freedom, yet ought not in all respects to be admitted to full fruition of the exemptions of the English and are still liable to the payment of taxes."[35]

As the 1668 Act clearly specified, English women were exempt from paying taxes on themselves or having their menfolk pay taxes on them. This was another distinction based on race. By obtaining tax relief for his womenfolk after experiencing a tragedy, Anthony effectively placed them on par with English women. By then, he and Mary had lived in Virginia for over thirty years.

When Anthony Johnson encountered John Casor in Northampton in front of Captain Goldsmith in 1653, Johnson was well acquainted with the English system regarding servitude. After releasing his servant under duress, he seems to have stewed over the Casor matter for months. While tending to his cows and crops on his two-hundred and fifty acres, he decided to sue Robert Parker for the loss of the services of John Casor.

Before a commissioner,[36] Johnson likely said, "I bring this complaint against Mr. Robert Parker for he hath detained one John Casor, a Negro who is my servant, under the pretense that said Casor is a freeman.[37] John Casor is my servant for life, and I seek his return."

"What say ye, Mr. Parker?" the commissioner probably asked the defendant.

"John Casor is a freeman, your honor. We discussed this before," likely replied Parker.

"But do you have his paper of indenture?" the commissioner probably asked.

"No, your honor, I do not."

"In that case, I order you to return the Negro John Casor to his right master Anthony Johnson."

Shock probably registered on Casor's and Parker's faces.

"It is my judgment," the commissioner probably continued, "that said Negro John Casor shall forthwith return into the service of his master Anthony Johnson and that said Mr. Robert Parker shall make payment of all court charges."[38]

Johnson and Casor battled over the latter's entitlement to liberty as a storm of injustice blew through the House of Burgesses. Casor ultimately gained his freedom in Maryland, where he raised his own livestock.[39] How and why he relocated to Maryland is not specifically known, but we can speculate that Maryland presented Casor's best chance to start over with a farm of his own.

Meanwhile, the legislative body enacted laws with devastating consequences for all subsequently abducted Africans brought to Virginia.

FIVE

*

Transforming Servitude

How did African immigrants descend from being considered as servants for limited terms, or indentured servants similar to their English compatriots, to becoming legally defined as servants for life, or slaves? Prior to 1670, Professor Russell noted, "The status of Africans who came or were brought to Virginia . . . was not determined by statute law either before or after that date."[1] As discussed, the 1624 to 1625 census designated twenty-three Africans, which included Anthony and Mary Johnson, in the Virginia colony as servants, and thus they received the same class name as many whites.[2] Likewise, county records created between 1632 and 1661 designate Blacks as "servants," "negro servants," or simply "negroes," but never as "slaves."[3] The answer to the legal transformation of Africans from servants to slaves seems to be rooted in both their increasing numbers and in the intermarrying and other sexual interactions between Africans and English.

The *White Lion* sailed into Virginia with the first "20 or odd Negroes," as John Rolfe described the ship's human cargo, and was followed closely by the *Treasurer* with about 30 Angolans aboard in 1619. We do not know how many Africans accompanied Anthony Johnson aboard the *James* in 1621 or landed with Mary Johnson aboard the *Margrett and John* in 1622. The website www.slavevoy ages.org contains a database with information about approximately 36,000 slaving voyages that transported Africans across the Atlantic.[4] The data for the USA begins in 1645 and ends in 1860 with an estimated total of 252,658 disembarkations during that period.[5] As depicted in Table 1-1, a total of 472,300 Africans were estimated to have arrived in British North America, which consisted of both the USA and Canada. The bottom line is that these voyages from Africa increased around the time that the Virginia legislature started making distinctions between the English and Africans.

The first legal reference to a Negro came in 1630 from the judicial proceedings of the governor and the council of Virginia, which ordered "Hugh Davis to be soundly whipped, before an assembly of Negroes and others for abusing himself to the dishonor of God and the shame of Christians by defiling his body in lying with a Negro, which fault he is to acknowledge next Sabbath day."[6] By the year 1630, Africans had been living in the Virginia colony for eleven years at a time when there were more English men than women. The governor and council seemed to believe that by ordering Hugh Davis "soundly whipped" he was supposed to abstain from sexual relations altogether rather than voluntarily having them with a Negro. The governor and council ordered Davis "soundly whipped" before an assembly of Negroes, but not before an assembly of English. Presumably this proclamation was to encourage other Negroes to refuse any attempts by Englishmen to lay with them.

Another possible interpretation of the 1630 order was that Hugh Davis might have raped the Negro woman. His sentence of being whipped in front of Negroes could have given the impression that Negro women had moral value, and their personal integrity was to be preserved.

June Purcell Guild, LLM, would probably have disagreed with the latter interpretation because she cites this case in the chapter called "The Struggle for Racial Integrity" in her book *The Black Laws of Virginia*.[7] This implies she believes that Davis was being punished for violating a previously unstated rule of copulating only with members of his own race so that any resulting children were purely English.

Guild next cites a 1640 incident in which Robert Sweet was ordered "to do penance in church according to the laws of England for impregnating a Negro woman with a child, and the woman whipped."[8] Sweet's child would be born a mulatto, with genetics equally English and African. Here was another instance of disparate treatment. Sweet was ordered to essentially pray and ask God's forgiveness whereas the African woman, whose name was not listed, was subjected to violence, which could have endangered the child that she was carrying.

In 1642, the Virginia House of Burgesses passed Chapter XX necessitating that "the consent of the master . . . be obtained for marriage. . . ." Its preamble suggests this law sought to curtail indentured servants from secretly marrying each other or from committing fornication. By doing either without first obtaining their master's consent, Chapter XX required that time be added to the indentured servant's contract, although it did not specify how much time. Fifteen years later, the House of Burgesses rectified this lapse by providing in Act XIV that "Servants marrying without the consent of their master are to serve one year after their term has expired."[9]

Freemen, or those who had already finished their indentured service to a master, were required to pay fines with tobacco for engaging in fornication. Because freemen no longer had a master, they could presumably marry women who had already finished their term of servitude. If a freeman married someone else's servant without her master's permission, however, he was required in Act XIV "to pay double the value of the extra service."[10] Should a freeman fornicate with another person's servant and impregnate her, he was required to give security to maintain the child. Such security could amount to paying 1,500 pounds of tobacco or giving one year of service to the woman's master.[11]

Virginia's House of Burgesses clearly felt it important to regulate sex between the English and Africans. It also deemed it urgent to limit marriages between servants to those approved of by masters.

Finally, it repeatedly outlawed what it considered the sins of "Adultery, whoredom, fornication, and drunkenness" in one bill and
those of "drunkenness, blasphemous cursing, swearing, adultery,
fornication" in another bill.[12] In the 1645 bill, individuals could be
"fined by county courts," and in the 1657 bill, the House of Burgesses specified the fines of fifty pounds of tobacco for first offense
drunkenness, twelve pounds of tobacco for swearing.[13]

In 1663, John Johnson, Anthony and Mary's son and a planter
in his own right, was charged with fornicating with a white woman
who lived on a neighboring plantation.[14] When Hannah Leach, a
servant to Edmund Scarborough, became pregnant, the court ar-
rested John Johnson[15] for violating laws prohibiting interracial
fornication. John Johnson's wife, Susanna, stood by him and petitioned local justices for his release from sheriff's custody. Her petition was granted, provided that Johnson "put in security to keep
the parish harmless from a base child begotten [of] the body of
Hannah Leach."[16] Johnson also had to obtain a wet nurse and post
bond to guarantee his future behavior, and Hannah Leach escaped
corporal punishment because Scarborough paid 1,000 pounds of
tobacco for her security.[17]

Repeated attempts to standardize human behavior, particularly
by discouraging sexual relations between the English and Africans,
eventually led to laws designating that legal status was to be based
on matrilineal heritage.[18] In 1662, the House of Burgesses promul-
gated that year's Act XII, which read, "Children got by an Englishman upon a Negro woman shall be bond or free according to the
condition of the mother. . . ."[19] Thus, this Act acknowledged that
Free Black women lived in the colony and that, should they produce
children with an English father, Free Black, or an enslaved African,
their children would be free. Free women, whether black or white,
gave birth to free children and enslaved women produced enslaved
children.[20] This was a major shift from patrilineal heritage in England, where male children inherited status from their fathers.

The House of Burgesses actually discussed whether to continue
patrilineal heritage before promulgating the major shift to matri-

lineal heritage. In 1662, it expressed concern that should a master's children automatically be freed from service that "might induce loose persons to lay all their bastards to their masters."[21] Act VI then proceeded to punish those women who did indeed produce children by their masters by ordering "each woman servant got with child by her master shall after her indenture is expired be sold for two years by the church wardens." Such a harsh law made no distinction between those women who might have voluntarily slept with their masters versus those who might have been forced into their masters' beds. This law applied to all indentured servants because no distinction was made on the basis of race.

Under these views, the legal status of the father was irrelevant. All the focus zeroed in on the status of the woman as the only person who could transfer status to her children. This 1662 legal shift was particularly onerous for enslaved black women who had no choice as to whether to accept or reject a master's sexual advances.

A white slave master who impregnated his black slaves produced more black slaves, which became his property. One of the most brutal examples of master rape with devastating consequences happened in 1831 when fugitive slave Margaret Garner killed her two-year old daughter rather than have her recaptured into slavery. As slavecatchers descended on the Ohio home of her brother, a Free Black, Garner had planned to kill her other three children who had also been fathered by her master. Ironically, Garner was charged and convicted of damaging her master's property and not with murder of a human being. She was convicted and ordered returned to her master under the Fugitive Slave Law. Her story was immortalized in the Tony Morrison's Pulitzer Prize-winning book *Beloved*, in a movie by the same name staring Oprah Winfrey as Garner, and in the 2005 Opera "Margaret Garner."[22]

Such was the desire to become a Free Black and escape the perils of slavery and lasciviousness of masters, Harriet Jacobs concealed herself in her grandmother's attic for seven years before she could finally journey through the Underground Railroad to the North. Jacobs narrated her life in *Incidents in the Life of a Slave Girl*.[23] After evading slave catchers in New York, Jacobs eventually became a Free Black in New England where she embraced her freedom.

Conversely, while masters were considering their own children as property to be disposed of as they pleased, white women who gave birth to a child by an enslaved black person produced a free person. The white woman could be punished with up to six months imprisonment without bail and ordered to pay fines for violating the anti-miscegenation laws and her mulatto children become indentured servants for a term of years until reaching a certain age. Nevertheless, the children eventually became free, rather than enslaved, blacks.

Thus the die of disparate treatment had been long cast by the time the House of Burgesses declared all subsequently arriving Africans to be servants for life, or slaves, if they were not Christian, in 1670. "An act declaring who should be slaves," according to Professor Russell, applied "to servants brought in by ship after 1670. The test of Christianity was to determine whether they should be servants for a limited term or servants for life."[24] This religious assessment only applied to subsequently arriving Africans, not to Europeans.

After this monumental change in the status of Africans in 1670, the House of Burgesses continued to regulate sex. Indeed, *from 1630*, when the House of Burgesses had ordered Hugh Davis whipped before an assembly of Negroes for engaging in interracial sex, *until 1967*, various Virginia legislatures passed at least sixteen statutes and other rules forbidding interracial sex and marriage.

For example, in 1691, the Virginia colonial legislature passed Act XVI to forbid intermarriage between people of color and whites. The specific Virginia legislation stated, "whatsoever English or other white man or woman, bond or free, shall intermarry with a Negro, mulatto, or Indian man or woman, bond or free, he shall within three months be banished from this dominion forever."[25] Consequently, within this time period if a free white person married a Free Black, they were both exiled from Virginia.

The Act stated that it was designed to prevent the "abominable mixture and spurious issue which hereafter may increase" as a result of such intermarriage.[26] Moreover, Act XVI, in 1691, provided that any free white woman who had "a bastard child by a Negro . . . shall pay fifteen pounds to the church wardens, and in default of such payment, she shall be taken into possession by the church wardens and disposed of for five years."[27] Her child could also "be bound out by the church wardens until he is thirty years of age." This Act XVI thus made both mother and child servants for a term.[28]

Since blacks and whites could not marry each other, these laws guaranteed the illegitimacy of any children resulting from such unions. The parents could be imprisoned, fined, or forced into indentured servitude. Depending on the status of the mother, the children were either enslaved or indentured for a term of years before obtaining their freedom. The harsh legal approach to the couple guaranteed that their children suffered by not being raised by parents who loved them and were genetically connected to them.

It was not until the Supreme Court decided *Loving v. Virginia*[29] in 1967 and struck down anti-miscegenation statutes in all fifty states that Virginia ceased criminalizing interracial sex. Margaret Jeter, a black woman, and Richard Loving, a white man, were residents of Virginia when they married in Washington, D.C., in 1958. They returned to Virginia and were charged with violating the anti-miscegenation statute. Their one-year jail sentence was suspended on the condition that they leave Virginia and not return for 25 years. In a unanimous decision, the Supreme Court found that distinctions drawn according to race were generally "odious to a free people" and that the Virginia law violated the Fourth Amendment. "[T]he Freedom to marry, or not marry, a person of another race resides with the individual and cannot be infringed by the State," according to the Court.

In the 337 years between the Hugh Davis whipping and the Lovings' banishment to avoid jail, countless numbers of other individuals were whipped, fined, imprisoned, or banned from Virginia for loving who they loved. Some individuals were probably even killed by unenlightened persons concerned about enforcing racial integrity.

The centuries of anti-miscegenation statutes amazes when one considers the number of different men throughout the decades who contributed to the writing of these statutes. It seems to have never dawned on any of them that the mere act of banning voluntary coupling, while ignoring master rape, actually led to more people to engage in miscegenation activities. As Mark Twain later proclaimed in *The Adventures of Tom Sawyer*, "To promise not to do a thing is the surest way in the world to make a body want to go and do that very thing."[30] Or, more specifically to Virginia, to ban an activity causes regulated individuals to desire to engage in that activity.

Meghan Carr Horrigan's article, *The State of Marriage in Virginia History: A Legislative Means of Identifying the Cultural Other*, argued that Virginians were passing these laws because they were less concerned with black women bearing mixed race children than they were with white women bearing mixed race children.[31] In both instances, the result was a child whose parents were black and white, but Horrigan maintained that Virginia viewed white women as the keepers of racial purity.[32] If white women were producing mulattos, then there were fewer purer English being added to the colony. By contrast, enslaved women producing mulattos augmented their masters' wealth.

The combination of basing status on matrilineal heritage and requiring that all subsequently arriving Africans after 1670 were to be considered slaves if they were not Christian dramatically curtailed the growth of the Free Black population while augmenting the numbers of the enslaved.

*

SIX

Restrictions on Population Growth and Civil Liberties

In addition to eliminating opportunities for subsequently arriving Africans to become indentured servants and eventually receive their freedom, Virginia legislatures also began circumscribing the growth of the Free Black population and their rights. These restrictions can be seen as efforts to eliminate the rights of slaveholders to manumit, or free, their slaves, to abridge civil liberties that landholding and other Free Blacks had enjoyed along with their white counterparts, and to tax Free Blacks in a manner divergent from taxing whites.

Despite decades of attempts to restrain interracial coupling and marriage, mulatto children became three of the five sources accounting for the continued growth of the Free Black population between 1670 and 1865. The designation of all subsequently arriving Africans as servants for life, if they were not Christian, essentially ended the possibility of African captives who voyaged across the Atlantic and landed in British North America to become indentured servants released after a term of years.

It seems unlikely that few Africans arrived from their tribes of origins having already been proselytized. Some of the post-1670 captives, like the original 1619 Africans who landed in Virginia, might have been baptized had they begun their journey on a Spanish ship before being kidnapped by an English one.[1] Even had they been taught Catholicism by the Portuguese, however, the Africans would not have won favor with the Protestants of English descent. Further, the language barrier curtailed the sharing of religious beliefs.

Once adherents to Catholicism, the English under Henry VIII had denounced the religion after the Pope refused to grant the king dispensation to divorce Catherine of Aragon, Henry VIII's first wife. Henry VIII created the Church of England as a Protestant alternative in 1534 and declared himself head of the church. He then married Anne Boleyn, who would become the mother of Elizabeth I before being the first of two of his six wives to be beheaded. Henry VIII and James I, for whom Jamestown was named, shared the common ancestor of Henry VII, who was the former's father and the latter's great-grandfather.

Certainly, there was no incentive for ship captains and their underlings to teach the Gospel contained in the *King James Bible* to their captives because slaves brought higher income on the auction block than indentured servants. Thus, the Free Black population primarily grew internally from Africans who were already in the colony and had received freedom prior to 1670. The Johnson family was not among those Free Blacks contributing to Virginia's population growth. Sometime in the 1680s, they left Virginia for Somerset, Maryland, where one of Anthony and Mary's grandsons named his farm "Angola."[2]

Professor Russell delineated five categories of Free Blacks added to the Virginia population: (1) black children born to Free Black parents; (2) mulatto children born to Free Black or mulatto mothers whose fathers were either indentured white servants, white freeman, or white landowners; (3) mulatto children born to white indentured servants or freewomen whose fathers were either black or mulatto enslaved men, indentured men, or freemen; (4) children born to Free Black and Indian mixed parents; and (5) manumitted slaves.[3] In Russell's first four categories, all the children were born to free mothers, whether they were black, white, or mulatto. These children benefited from matrilineal heritage that designated child status based on the status of their mothers. Births to free mothers were the primary avenue of Free Black population growth during this segment of Virginia's colonial history.

As for the third category Professor Russell mentioned—mulatto children born to white mothers—the Virginia legislature passed a law in 1705 stating that indentured women servants who had illegitimate children by a Negro or mulatto were liable for a fine or could be sold as a servant for five years at the expiration of their original indenture.[4] Her children were to be bound out as servants until the age of thirty-one.[5] By 1765, the legislature had lowered the term and required that the illegitimate boys of women servants and blacks, or of free Christian white women by blacks, were to be bound out until they reached age twenty-one.[6] Illegitimate girls became indentured servants until they reached the age of eighteen.[7]

It was the fifth category that required legal action on the part of the slave owner, and the right was either permitted or prohibited depending on legislative enactments. A slaveholder had to file a deed during his or her life to set someone free or could do so in a last will and testament. The American Revolution eventually increased the category of manumitted slaves, but only for a time.

* * * * *

Restrictions on Manumissions

As the population of Free Blacks grew significantly from births to free women in the seventeenth and eighteenth centuries, Virginia legislators became so concerned about the increasing number of Free Blacks in their territory that they adopted laws prohibiting private manumission of slaves.[8] Laws enacted between 1691 and 1745, which became effective through the end of the Revolutionary War, limited the increase of Free Blacks "to natural means and to manumissions by special legislative acts."[9]

Virginia's 1691 Act XVI can be broken into three sections. First, the legislature noted, "A great inconvenience may happen to this country by the setting of Negroes and mulattoes free, by their entertaining Negroes from their masters' service, or receiving stolen goods, or being grown old bringing a charge upon the country, it is enacted that no Negroes, or mulattoes be set free by any person whatsoever." Second, the legislature mandated that manumitting masters "pay for transportation of such Negro out of the country within six months after such setting free" a slave.[10] Third, the legislature imposed fines for violators, or a "penalty of ten pounds sterling to the church wardens, with which the church wardens are to cause the Negro to be transported out of the country and the remainder given to the use of the poor of the parish."[11]

This incredibly harsh Act imagined the horrors of adding to the Free Black population through manumission, including that a Free Black might entertain another master's slaves and thus, perhaps, encourage them to imagine their freedom to come and go as they pleased. Both Solomon Northup's book *12 Years a Slave*, and the film by the same name, depict an example of such through the story of the slave Patsey's visit to Master Shaw's black wife, Harriet, without receiving permission from Master Epps to leave his plantation.[12] Patsey was in the unenviable position of being desired by Master Epps and despised by Mrs. Epps because of her husband's relationship with the unwilling Patsey. When confronted by Master Epps about her whereabouts, Patsey explained that she only went over to the Shaw house because "Missus don't give me soap to wash with, as she does the rest."[13] Despite her efforts to keep herself clean, a suspicious and jealous Epps ordered Solomon Northup to whip Patsey to discourage her from going to the Shaw House for fear that the white master Shaw might have designs on his black Patsey.[14]

Another horror the 1691 Act envisioned was that Free Blacks might receive goods stolen from masters. Many masters were known to inventory their goods,[15] which should have eased such a fear.

The final concern was that Free Blacks might grow old and "bring a charge upon the country."[16] Masters were required to care for their slaves even when they could no longer work. Indeed, in 1661 the Virginia legislature had passed CIII to require that "every master shall provide servants with competent diet, clothing, [and] lodging."[17] The 1691 Act seemed to express legislative concern that with no masters to care for them, Free Blacks could not maintain and sustain themselves during their elder years.

On the mere possibility that some enslaved person might steal from a master, the 1691 Act proclaimed that no master could free a slave unless he transported the person out of the colony within six months. The 1691 Act did not totally prohibit a master from freeing a slave because he could do so as long as he was willing to transport the Free Black out of the colony within six months. This placed an additional expense upon the master to remove the individual and potentially provided a hardship upon the individual who might become separated from family members who remained enslaved. The 1691 Act imposed a penalty upon masters who did not transport their newly freed slaves out of the country of ten pounds sterling payable to the church wardens. It then became the duty of the church wardens to transport the newly freed slave out of the country. The 1691 Act sought to guarantee that no newly Free Blacks remained within Virginia. This was in keeping with the Virginia Legislature's proclamations that the Free Black population should only grow by "natural means," or births to free women who were already citizens of Virginia.

In 1723, the Virginia legislature eliminated the freedom to manumit slaves even if they were transported out of the country within six months. Chapter IV abolished private deeds of manumission that by providing, "No Negro or Indian slave shall be set free upon any pretence whatsoever, except for some meritorious services, to be [adjudicated] by the governor and council, and a license thereupon obtained."[18] This Act prohibited property owners from having complete fee simple ownership in their human property. A normal fee simple included the power to alienate property by giving it away, including the gifting of freedom to slaves.

After the passage of Chapter IV, the only path for slaves to join the Free Black population was by a public act of emancipation for what the governor and council deemed as "meritorious service." This 1723 statute was so arduous that it further asserted, "If a slave is set free otherwise than as directed, the church wardens are required to take up and sell the individual as a slave by public outcry and the monies shall be applied to the use of the parish."[19] Not only was there no separation from church and state at this time, but the two were entrenched because the legislature used the church wardens as their marshals to enforce legislative decrees. Thus, any attempt at private manumission resulted in the church wardens reselling a newly freed person into slavery. This was the harshest punishment of all because the acquiring master was unlikely to be as benevolent as the freedom-granting one.

Statutes providing that someone could be freed for "meritorious service" did in reality lead the Virginia legislature to enact such measures freeing a few blacks. In 1710, for example, the Virginia legislature passed a law setting free Will for his service in helping to disrupt a slave conspiracy.[20] Chapter XVI in that year provided, "Whereas a Negro slave named Will, belonging to Robt. Ruffin, of the County of Surry, was signally serviceable in discovering a conspiracy of Negroes for levying war in this colony; for a reward of his fidelity, it is enacted that the said Will is and forever hereafter shall be free and shall continue to be within his colony, if he think fit to continue. The sum of forty pounds sterling shall be paid the said Robt. Ruffin for the price of Will."[21]

The actions of Will viewed by the colonial legislature as meritorious were probably seen as treacherous by other enslaved blacks. Mr. Robert Ruffin doubly benefitted from Will's actions since the insurrection was stopped and he was reimbursed for the loss of Will's service to him. Should Will have chosen to stay in Virginia in 1711, the slaves whose rebellion was squashed probably treated him as a snitch and ostracized him. Probably those planning insurrection were severely punished or hung. At that time, the legislature may have practiced what they enshrined into law in 1748 with Chapter XXXVIII, which stated, "The conspiracy of slaves or their insurrection is a felony and the penalty death without benefit of clergy."[22]

In 1779 the legislature declared that a "slave named Kitt, owned by Hinchia Mabry, of Brunswick, has rendered meritorious service in making the first information against several counterfeiters, and is hereby emancipated and his owner ordered paid 1,000 pounds out of the public treasury."[23]

Since slaves were considered valuable property, setting them free potentially involved financial sacrifice. Similar to what happened to Will, the legislature purchased the freedom of a slave named Kitt because he exposed counterfeiters.[24] Kitt probably saved the treasury more money than was likely expensed in paying his master for his freedom. Whether the counterfeiters were white or black was never specifically stated by the Act.

After the Revolutionary War, these various Acts prohibiting private manumission were repealed or amended. Starting in 1782, some Africans who were servants for life were granted their freedom through deeds and wills.

The ultimate act of public freeing of slaves occurred with the Emancipation Proclamation which proposed to set free all southern enslaved blacks on January 1, 1863. The Emancipation Proclamation read, in part,

That on the first day of January, in the year of our Lord one thousand eight hundred and sixty-three, all persons held as slaves within any State or designated part of a State, the people whereof shall then be in rebellion against the United States, shall be then, thenceforward, and forever free; and the Executive Government of the United States, including the military and naval authority thereof, will recognize and maintain the freedom of such persons, and will do no act or acts to repress such persons, or any of them, in any efforts they may make for their actual freedom.

It was signed by President Abraham Lincoln and Secretary of State William H. Seward. The Proclamation did not apply to slaves held in the North because they were not in rebellion.[25] In 1865, the United States passed the Thirteenth Amendment to free all men and women held in bondage throughout the entire country, including those who had remained enslaved in the North.

* * * * *

Abolishing Freedom of Assembly, Carrying Arms, and Voting Rights

Ten years after the momentous statute that changed the status of subsequently arriving Africans, the House of Burgesses passed Act X in 1680 to abolish the rights of blacks to peacefully assemble. It deplored "the frequent meetings of considerable numbers of Negro slaves under pretense of feasts and burials."[26] By declaring such meetings as "dangerous,"[27] the legislators were probably concerned that they could provide cover for planning insurrections.

The same Act X prohibited all blacks, both the free and the enslaved, from carrying "arms, such as any club, staff, gun, sword, or other weapon."[28] Slaves also could not leave their owners' plantations "without a certificate and then only on necessary occasions."[29] Failure to have such written permission when traveling from a plantation led to the punishment of "twenty lashes on the bare back, well laid on."[30] Thus, legislators envisioned blacks being brutally whipped for violating these restrictions on their freedom of assembly and of movement. In his book, *In the Matter of Color*, Higginbotham compared the requirement that blacks carry papers, or a certificate, to devices employed by "despotic governments."[31]

In 1723, the Virginia colonial legislature abolished voting rights for Free Blacks and Indians, after they had possessed these rights for over a century.[32] The 1723 Act specifically stated, "No free Negro or Indian whatsoever shall hereafter have any vote at any election."[33] Like many legal rights, others are presumed to have them until they are specifically removed. While there remains no legislative record as to what motivated the change, perhaps the legislators dehumanized blacks and Indians with comments such as, "there are too many of them," or "there are more of them than there are of us."

The right to vote is one of the cornerstones of civil liberties, particularly in a representative democracy. That Free Blacks and Indians had the right to suffrage for over a century is a little known fact in this country. Black men were eventually legally enfranchised by the passage of the Fifteenth Amendment to the Constitution.[34] The Fifteenth Amendment to the Constitution[35] declared that "[t]he right of citizens of the United States to vote shall not be denied or abridged by the United States or by any state on account of race, color, or previous condition of servitude." It was ratified on February 3, 1870.

Black women were ostensibly empowered to vote with the ratification of the Nineteenth Amendment to the U.S. Constitution on August 18, 1920, which granted the liberty to all women. However, it took the events accompanying the Civil Rights struggle in Selma, Alabama, before the United States Congress passed the Voting Rights Act in 1965[36] to fully implement the power of the ballot for black men and women.

According to the United States Justice Department website, "The Voting Rights Act, adopted initially in 1965 and extended in 1970, 1975, and 1982," remains "the most successful piece of civil rights legislation ever adopted by the United States Congress."[37] In addition, the Act codifies and effectuates the 15th Amendment's permanent guarantee that, throughout the nation, no person shall be denied the right to vote on account of race or color, and "contains several special provisions that impose even more stringent requirements in certain jurisdictions throughout the country."[38]

With the passage of the decades, the Voting Rights Act of 1965 came under attack from those seeking another era of retrenchment from this most important civil liberty. In 2013, for example, the U.S. Supreme Court struck down Section 4(b) on the coverage formula as unconstitutional in *Shelby County v. Holder*, 133 S. Ct. 2612, 2651 (2013).[39] Remembering that Free Black male landowners had the right to vote up until 1723 urges the preservation of suffrage. Once enfranchisement is lost, centuries may pass before it is regained. After Indians lost the right to vote in 1723, they did not fully reacquire suffrage throughout the entire country until 1969. With the passage of 246 years, Indians were no longer the majority of the people on the North American continent.

✳ ✳ ✳ ✳ ✳

Taxing Blacks and Indians

Another area where Virginia legislatures enacted laws with disparate treatment between whites and people of color, and between men and women, centered on taxation. While masters paid taxes on all of their slaves,[40] Free Blacks and white men paid personal taxes. No taxes were assessed on white women, possibly because there was a shortage of them from the beginnings of the Virginia colony. Recall what happened to Anthony Johnson after a fire destroyed part of his property when he successfully sought relief from paying taxes on his wife Mary and their two daughters.[41] This was an exception to the rule that required the payment of taxes on Free Black women.

The 1668 Act VII reaffirmed the divergent gender and racial taxation treatment by providing, "Negro women though permitted to enjoy their freedom, yet ought not in all respects to be admitted to full fruition of the exemptions of the English and are still liable to the payment of taxes."[42] This Act acknowledged the existence of Free Black women while stating specifically that they were not on equal status to white women who did not have to pay taxes on themselves or have their menfolk do so. Although they might share freedom with white women, black women were constantly reminded that they were not equal to their white counterparts.

Initially, human property was compared to realty[43] and later to personal property.[44] Slaves were considered the most valuable property after realty. In 1705, Act VII provided, "It is enacted that all male persons of the age of sixteen years and upward, and all Negro, mulatto, and Indian women of sixteen years, not being free shall be tithable or chargeable for defraying the public, county, and parish charges in this her majesty's colony and dominion, excepting such only as the county court and vestry for reasons in charity shall think fit to excuse."[45] Further, "Every master or mistress shall, under penalty, by a list cause to be delivered to the justice the name of all tithable persons belonging to his or her family."[46] The tax, in part, supported charity for those who were unable to care for themselves.

The allusion to her majesty in this legislation refers to Queen Anne, who ruled England from 1702 to 1714. Her father was James II, a grandson of James I. Since Anne died without surviving issue, despite having endured seventeen pregnancies, she was the last monarch of the House of Stuart, whose reign began with James I. This Act considered the taxes collected on all men over the age of sixteen and all women of color over the age of sixteen as helping defray public charges. In 2018, Queen Anne received cinematic treatment in *The Favourite*[47] and the origin story of James I was told in *Mary Queen of Scots*.[48] *The Favourite* depicts many disputes about increasing taxes on Anne's subjects. During Anne's reign, those subjects included Free Blacks, enslaved Africans, and English men in Virginia, all of whom, according to Act VII, were taxed to support her government and its various wars.

In 1705, an additional Chapter XXIII was enacted to provide, "All Negro, mulatto, and Indian slaves within this dominion shall be held to be real estate and not chattels and shall descend unto heirs and widows according to the custom of land inheritance, and be held in fee simple."[49] This chapter confirmed inheritance rights in slaves. Further, the Act provided "that any merchant bringing slaves into this dominion shall hold such slaves whilst they remain unsold as personal estate. All such slaves may be taken on execution as other chattels; slaves shall not be escheatable."[50]

Modern folks might find all of these taxes reprehensible, particularly that slaves were initially compared to land, which is immovable, and not chattels, which are movables. At the time, land passed to heirs under the English law of primogeniture, by which estates descended from father to eldest son. Primogeniture and the practice of entail, which also kept landed estates in families for generations, was not be completely abolished in Virginia until the late 1770s.[51] Chattels, or personal property, however, could be divided among the father's other children. Either method of comparison reinforced that slaves were considered property that could be taxed by the government, sold to others in fee simple, or inherited.

In her book *Incidents in the Life of a Slave Girl*, Harriot Jacobs discussed the reading of her mistress's will, in which the mistress bequeathed Jacobs to her sister's daughter, a child of five years old.[52] That was how Jacobs came to live with the lascivious Dr. Flint, who had married the sister of Jacobs' mistress, and from whom she escaped.

The phrase "escheatable" references the normal right of the state to take property if heirs cannot be found. Under this provision, the territory of Virginia forfeited the right to receive slaves if heirs could not be found, but the provision did not indicate what happened to such slaves, such as whether they were granted their freedom. For example, in 1810 the Virginia legislature set free a widow and the children of Frank, a Free Black, who had died and left his family in bondage.[53] The law provided, "A certain free man of color, by the name of Frank, has died, leaving in bondage a widow, Patience, and three children, whom Frank, by meritorious industry, purchased in his lifetime, but failed to emancipate; it is enacted by the General Assembly that Patience and the children shall be free."[54]

Frank probably did not free Patience and their children because they would have been forced to leave the state. Rather than have Patience and Frank's children belong to the state, the Virginia legislature chose to release them from bondage. The legislature thus chose to honor Frank's industriousness which enabled him to purchase his family in the first place. Within his household unity, Frank probably treated his family as humans and not as his property.

A different generation of Virginia legislators passed the 1723 Chapter IV to further proclaim, "All free Negroes, mulattoes, and

Indians (except tributary Indians to this government), male and female above sixteen years of age, and all wives of such, shall be deemed tithables,"[55] or taxable. Though the people had changed, their taxation intent had not. Continuing to tax individuals, rather than their income or wealth, seemed an unusual method of assessing taxes, which was based on an individual's status rather than his or her income.

Twenty-five years later, the Virginia legislature slightly changed its taxation approach. It enacted Chapter II in 1748 to provide, "Negroes having been declared to be real estate in 1705 and afterward this explained by act in 1727 and the acts having been found inconvenient, they are repealed, and for the future all slaves shall be taken to be chattels."[56] The 1748 Act thus transformed human property from being compared to land (an immovable) to chattels (or movables). This probably led more groups of slaves to be divided among the masters' children rather than be given as a large group to one son. To effect an even division of slaves, some were sold with the revenue divided between the masters' children. Slave families were then dispersed beyond immediate families, possibly eliminating the hope of occasionally seeing relatives. This change was brought about because the government found it "inconvenient" to continue taxing humans using the real estate comparison method.

Regarding enslaved women, both wills and deeds referred to their potential children as "future increase." The will of J. John Pinick of the County of Prince Edward, for example, gave his son Thomas "one Negro girl named Hannah and all her future increase."[57] Similarly, John Willis of Amelia County gifted his sister "One negro girl named Hannah, with future increase."[58] The deed recorded on August 22, 1782, further specified that this gift was part of Aggatha's share of their deceased father's estate, and upon Aggatha's death, Hannah's increase was "to be equally [distributed] to her children."[59] In this deed to effect the division of an estate's contents, Pinick seemed to take no notice that he and his family were divvying up human beings into a future generation.

As indicated by these references in wills and deeds, the century and decades following the 1670 monumental status change defining Africans as servants for life brought increased dehumanization of the enslaved alongside the further erosion of rights for Free Blacks.

*

SEVEN

The Revolutionary War's Impact
on Free Blacks

From 1619, when the first Africans landed in Virginia, until to 1781, when the last major battle of the Revolutionary War was fought at Yorktown, all Free Blacks, enslaved blacks, and whites in Virginia were the subjects of ten monarchs (James I, Charles I, Charles II, James II, William III and Mary II, Anne, George I, George II, and George III). Jamestown was named after the first of these British sovereigns and George III was the sovereign from whom the colonists rebelled. Virginia received its name to honor Elizabeth I, the self-proclaimed Virgin Queen.

Ironically, given the prior chapter's conversation about the personal taxation of the colony's Free Blacks, enslaved blacks, and white men, what motivated the rebellion against England was its taxation of the colonies. Like his predecessors (recall the earlier reference to her majesty, Queen Anne, in one taxation statute), George III and his parliament saw the colonies as sources of revenue. If the kingdom needed more funds to finance its wars, such as the ultimate victory over the French in the seven year's French and Indian War, Parliament raised taxes on the colonies.

Parliament passed The Stamp Act in 1765 during the reign of

George II, the grandfather of George III, to require nearly everything written on paper, other than private correspondence and books, to "carry revenue stamps, some costing as much as ten pounds."[1] The Stamp Act applied to "all pamphlets, newspapers, advertisements, deeds, diplomas, bills, bonds, all legal documents, ship's papers, even playing cards."[2] Bostonians responded by first stoning the residence of Andrew Oliver, the secretary of the province who had been appointed distributor of the stamp.[3] Then, they destroyed the house of Lieutenant Governor Thomas Hutchinson, who they wrongly suspected of having sponsored the detested tax.[4]

Virginia was reported by the *Boston Gazette* as "in a state of 'utmost consternation'" because of the Stamp Act.[5] In Virginia's General Assembly toward the end of May 1765, Patrick Henry pontificated in favor of six resolutions objecting to the tax.[6] Four of the decrees passed, one of which by only one vote, and two failed.[7] After word reach England of the colonies' consternation about the law, Parliament repealed the Stamp Act in 1766. Simultaneously, it passed the Declaratory Act, which "stated its rights to pass laws, on any subject, that were binding on colonies."[8] The government of his majesty, George III, followed up with a tax on tea, to which the colonists reacted even more forcefully.

George III and his parliament members were no doubt shocked to receive the news that Bostonians had destroyed the highly taxed imported English tea belonging to the East India Company in December 1773. The Bostonians lightly camouflaged themselves as Indians before boarding three British vessels in the Boston Harbor. By one account, they "hauled hundreds of tea casks to deck, smashed them open, and dumped their contents into the harbor—forty-five tons of tea, enough to litter the beaches for miles and depress the company's profits for years."[9]

The incident became known as the Boston Tea Party, for the colonists' first major retaliation against the increased taxes on tea. Lord North, the British prime minister, spearheaded the decision to punish Massachusetts people by passing the Coercive Acts of 1774, which triggered the ensuing war, according to historian Andrew

Jackson O'Shaughnessy, author of *The Men Who Lost America*.[10] Lord North was once described as having "Two large prominent eyes that rolled about to no purpose."[11]

Challenging the English government's taxation authority brought uncertainty and fear within all thirteen colonies. As John Adams wrote to his wife Abigail in 1774, "We live, my dear soul, in an age of trial. What will be the consequence, I know not."[12] While the First Continental Congress was meeting in 1774, King George III declared, "The dye is now cast, the Colonies must either submit or triumph."[13]

The colonists accepted the challenge. Between 1774 and 1776, historian Andrew Jackson O'Shaughnessy wrote, "the revolutionaries successfully took over control of the apparatus of government, including the assemblies, councils, court system, and local authorities, as well as the press."[14]

On June 19, 1775, at its meeting in Philadelphia, the Continental Congress commissioned George Washington, the tallest man it the room and who wore a Virginia Militia Colonel's uniform, to lead the Continental Army. This war-time grouping of men was known as "the army of the United Colonies," "the troops under [Washington's] command," the "Troops of the United Provinces of North America," and by Washington's description as "raw materials" for an army.[15] Out-manned, out-gunned, and under-paid, the Continental Army confronted His Majesty's well-trained and highly-resourced troops.

Free Blacks immediately joined and fought alongside whites[16] during the initial battles of the Revolutionary War at Lexington, Concord, and the Battle of Bunker Hill. Washington, who had been initially resistant to the idea of letting blacks fight besides whites, relented. Simply put, he needed more men. Having observed some of the early enlistees fight with courage, on December 31, 1775, George Washington wrote a letter to the Continental Congress requesting permission to allow Free Blacks to reenlist with its approval.[17] This was an integrated army, with whites and blacks fighting together, and remained so for most of the war, until a few "colored regiments [were] formed in 1777, primarily in the southern colonies."[18]

In July 1776 as concerns increased about English practices of imposing taxes without receiving input from the colonies, Virginia's Thomas Jefferson became the primary author of the Declaration of Independence. His goal was to tie together "all of the colonists' grievances—some more serious than others—creating a united front."[19] The Declaration of Independence proclaimed George III "a Tyrant" who was "unfit to be a ruler of people." He probably did not see himself this way, particularly since the primary constitutional role of the English sovereign after the fall of James II's reign in 1688 was to appoint a prime minster supported by the majority party.[20]

One of the first major battles of the Revolutionary War after the Declaration of Independence led to massive defeat for the Continental Army in Brooklyn, New York, on August 27, 1776.[21] The last major contest was fought at Yorktown, Virginia, on October 19, 1781, after which British General Cornwallis surrendered his army to a combined American and French force under Washington and Rochambeau. In the intervening years, Washington waged guerilla warfare for the bulk of the conflict. His only hope of success was to hold the Continental Army together until the British will collapsed.[22] The Chinese war thinker Sun Tzu had written about 2000 years before, "[T]o fight and conquer in all your battles is not supreme excellence; supreme excellence consists in breaking the enemy's resistance without fighting."[23]

In their efforts to eradicate the British desire for war, the rag-tag American forces suffered catastrophes. The British conquest of Philadelphia led the Continental Army to retreat to Valley Forge, Pennsylvania.[24] While wintering in Valley Forge from 1777–1778, the lack of supplies caused Washington's men to eat their horses and track bleeding bare feet in the snow. According to historian Andrew Jackson O'Shaughnessy, "The number of his troops fit for duty dropped from 14,122 in December 1777 to 7,316 in March 1778."[25] This represented a decline of able-bodied troops of almost fifty percent. Lieutenant Colonel Aaron Burr, then twenty-one years old, endured the horrific experiences of Valley Forge along with those men under his control.[26]

As members of the Continental Army, Free Blacks and Indians also suffered injuries and casualties in the war. Surprisingly, according to historian Benjamin Quarles, "The New England states, despite their relatively small Negro population, "probably furnished more colored soldiers than any other section."[27] "In central Massachusetts in 1777," Quarles added, "an observer reported that he ran across no regiment without 'a lot of Negroes'. In Connecticut practically no town of any sized failed to supply one or more Negroes for the Continental forces. Ten of Stratford's 114 soldiers were colored, as were 13 of Wallington's 132. The Rhode Island First Regiment enrolled some two hundred Negroes."[28]

The British offered freedom to slaves who fought on their side and treated other slaves as neutrals so long as they did not actively take up arms against them.[29] In the lead-up to the war on November 7, 1775, the Earl of Dunmore and Governor-General of the Virginia Colony, issued a proclamation that freed "all [indentured] Servants, Negroes or others . . . able and willing to bear Arms. . ." with His Majesty's troops.[30] At least twenty-three of the men, women and children Thomas Jefferson held in bondage answered Dunmore's call, for Jefferson noted in his Farm Book that they ran away from Monticello and "joined the enemy."[31] By 1778, thousands of slaves sought freedom in fighting behind the British lines, and thousand left with the Redcoats at the end of the conflict.[32] Striving for freedom led blacks to put their lives at risk on both sides.

In the southern colonies, some Free Blacks were drafted and some enslaved blacks were volunteered into service to replace their masters. While Maryland drafted Free Blacks and authorized slave enlistments, Free Blacks voluntarily enlisted in the Virginia army and navy.[33] A Free Black man named William Clark enlisted from his home in Virginia around 1776. Clark served as "a courier and fought at a number of battles, including Germantown and Monmouth."[34] Following the war's conclusion, he swore several oaths of his service, and both Clark and his wife Hannah were eventually granted a Revolutionary War pension.[35]

Delaware and North Carolina permitted slaves to serve in place of their masters.[36] Many of the slaves received freedom after the conflict ended, but some did not when their masters reneged on personal promises to manumit them from bondage. As the Supreme Court later wrote in the infamous *Dred Scott* case, "Slaves ... had no rights which the white man was bound to respect."[37] The slaves had no legal right to enforce their masters' promises even though they had placed themselves in the line of British bullets to fulfill their end of the bargain.

The New York General Assembly behaved more honorably than some of the southern masters who did not fulfil promises to their slaves. It authorized the enlistment of slaves in the Continental Army and promised them their freedom if they served for three years and their masters 500 acres of unappropriated public land for each slave delivered and enlisted.[38] Those slaves who fought for New York in the Continental Army technically received their freedom in 1781 at the conclusion of the war at Yorktown, but were forced to wait until 1785 for the New York General Assembly to complete their legal emancipation.

In 1785, Aaron Burr, by then a New York Senator, introduced a bill proposing the immediate and unconditional end of slavery for all blacks, but that bill was rejected 33 to 13 in favor of a gradual emancipation plan that passed by 36 to 11.[39] This final bill, which Burr opposed,[40] restricted civil liberties by providing that blacks could not vote, hold political office, intermarry with whites, or testify against whites in any court in the state.[41]

With the passage of this Act, Free Blacks in New York became on par with their compatriots in Virginia, possessing some civil liberties, but not all. For example, Virginia passed a law in 1785 that said "No Negro or mulatto shall be a witness, except in actions against Negroes, or in civil pleas wherein Negroes shall be parties."[42]

Nevertheless, the willingness of slaves and Free Blacks to fight in the Revolutionary War effort brought a measure of freedom to all blacks in New York, and impacted the lives of blacks by dramatically increasing the Free Black population in Virginia and other states. Harriet Beecher Stowe, the author of *Uncle Tom's Cabin*, observed

that these blacks who fought for "a nation which did not acknowledge them as citizens and equals" demonstrated bravery, which "under such circumstances, has a peculiar beauty and merit."[43]

* * * * *

The Free Black Population Census in the
United States and Virginia

Following the conclusion of the war, the Constitutional Convention
signed a constitution on September 17, 1787, mandating a decennial census in Article 1, Section 2. The first census was taken in 1790.
When the United States undertook that census, it revealed that
there were nearly 60,000 Free Blacks living in the United States as
indicated in Table 7-1. Within ten years, the population had nearly
doubled to over 108,000 and tripled to over 186,000 by 1810. Table
7-1 reveals another interesting fact: more Free Blacks lived in the
South than in the North between 1790 and 1810, and that fact never
changed throughout the entire antebellum period.

TABLE 7-1. Free Black Population, 1755–1810[44]

Territory	1755	1790	1800	1810
United States		59,466	108,395	186,446
North		27,109	47,154	78,181
South		32,357	61,241	108,265
Maryland	1,817	8,043	19,587	33,927
Virginia	1,800	12,886[45]	20,124	30,570

By 1810, forty-two percent of the all Free Blacks resided in the
northern United States while fifty-eight percent lived in the South.
    Table 7-2 depicts the proportion of blacks who were free as a per-
centage of total blacks in a particular location. Within the United
States in 1790, nearly eight percent of all blacks were free while the

other ninety-two percent of their brethren remained enslaved. By 1810, the number of Free Blacks as a percentage of overall blacks in the United States had risen to nearly fourteen, leaving over eighty-six percent enslaved.

TABLE 7-2. Proportion of Blacks Who Were Free, 1755–1810[46]

Territory	1755	1790	1800	1810
United States		7.9%	10.8%	13.5%
North		40.2%	56.7%	74%
South		4.7%	6.7%	8.5%
Maryland	4.0%	7.2%	15.6%	23.3%
Virginia	3.5%	7.3%	12%	18%

Table 7-2 further reveals that in Virginia, by contrast, only three and a half percent of all blacks were free in 1755, compared to the approximately ninety-six per cent who were enslaved. The decline in the percentage of Free Blacks proved that the 1670 status change, and the impediments to private manumissions of the enslaved, reduced the population growth because it was confined to "natural increase." By 1790 and eight years following the lifting the ban on private manumissions, those numbers had doubled to over seven percent of blacks who were free in Virginia whereas about ninety-three percent remained in bondage. Even though fewer Free Blacks were located in the North, that region had a higher percentage of blacks who were free residing there. The percent rose to seventy-four by 1810, which meant that only twenty-four percent of blacks living in the North remained enslaved.

Among the states, Delaware had the highest percentage of blacks who were free at seventy-six percent, whereas Mississippi possessed the lowest percentage of blacks who were free at barely over one percent. Master Shaw's black wife Harriet, who was depicted in Solomon Northup's *12 Years a Slave,*[47] was among those.

Why did more Free Blacks choose to reside in the South? It could be that the place of their birth was most familiar and felt like home. The distances were immense when one considers that people either walked or traveled by horse, buggy, stagecoach, or boat during this time. Perhaps, the most important considerations were the legal restrictions imposed on their freedom of movement, even for such purposes as obtaining an education. Virginia did eventually prohibit any "free person of color who shall migrate from the state, or who shall for the purpose of being educated be sent from the state, or who shall for any purpose go to a non-slaveholding state, shall be no longer entitled to residence in Virginia."[48] It appears that Virginia perceived educated blacks to be as much or even more "dangerous" than the enslaved who gathered for feasts and funerals, because educated Free Blacks lost their residency.

Additionally, other states passed laws stating that if their Free Blacks left the state, they could not return.[49] Indeed, Free Blacks faced whipping (39 lashes), imprisonment and fines if they returned after having been removed from Virginia.[50]

In a reprehensible action following the conclusion of the Revolutionary War in which many Free Blacks fought in the Virginia army and navy as well as the military regiments of other colonies, Virginia forbade Free Blacks from entering their territory from other states.[51] In 1793, the legislature passed Chapter 23 to provide, "This act forbids free Negroes or mulattoes from migrating into the Commonwealth. If they come in, they may be exported to the place from which they came."[52] Further, the act required, "Every Master of a vessel or other persons who shall bring into this Commonwealth by water or by land any free Negro shall forfeit one hundred pounds, one-half of to the Commonwealth and the other half to the informer."[53]

Virginia applied these limitations on movement to Free Blacks and slaves for decades. Indeed, the stated policy goal was outlined in Chapter XXVI, when passed in 1819, to limit the slaves and Free Blacks in the Commonwealth as to those in residence "on October 17, 1785 and the descendants of the females, and such slaves."[54] From that year forward, masters had to obtain legislative permission to bring slaves into the commonwealth. The legislature allowed Frances D. Tucker to bring her female slave Sally into the state because Frances sustained "considerable inconvenience on account of the loss of her services."[55] It also granted Thomas Woodford and Robert P. Montgomery leave to bring slaves back from Kentucky, and Perryn Caldwell and Henry Hines to both hold eight slaves brought from North Carolina.[56] The list of those states from which white slaveholders sought to bring in slaves also included Maryland and Alabama.[57] In every instance, the hopeful slaveholder had to obtain consent from the Virginia legislature.

Fifteen years later in 1834, Virginia amplified the penalties forbidding Free Blacks from entering its territory by imposing violence. The legislature passed Chapter 68 to provide, "A free Negro shall not migrate into this Commonwealth from any state in the Union, or from any foreign country, under penalty of thirty-nine lashes on his bare back at the public whipping post."[58] Those returning after removal were to be punished according to the act of 1819, and special fines and penalties were set for masters of vessels who bring in any free Negroes. The exception was made for travelers who had "any free Negroes in their employment."[59] If known to Free Blacks, such legislation encouraged those who were in Virginia to stay put and not leave, and those who were from other states to not journey to the Old Dominion.

Enslaved and Free Blacks fought and died during the Revolutionary War. The enslaved soldiers who survived to become emancipated by public proclamation or manumitted by private deed became Free Blacks. Their lives changed from containing no privileges to possessing the limited rights of those who were free with black skin.

EIGHT

*

Manumissions and Status Changes

Both immediately before and following the Revolutionary War, the movement to permit manumissions increased. The arguments for freeing slaves were based on religious grounds and on secular concerns about keeping others oppressed after the whites fought and obtained their freedom from England.[1]

The Quakers and the Methodists were at the forefront of the religious movement to repeal restrictions on manumission.[2] Professor Russell maintained, "Many Quakers in Virginia had been owners of slaves up to the period of the Revolutionary War, but they were among the first to recognize and admit fully the humanity of the [N]egro and the injustice of depriving him of his right to freedom."[3] Many Methodists, like the Quakers, "refused to own or sell slaves."[4] These spiritual changes affected some Virginia slaveholders and increased their demand for the right to set their slaves free, if they wished. Indeed, as historian Ron Chernow wrote, "Among many Americans, the Revolution had generated a backlash against slavery as a horrifying practice incompatible with Republican ideals."[5]

Slaveholders also protested against the prohibition on manumission as affecting their property rights.[6] The Virginia protests, according to Professor Russell, arose because the prohibition was

65

considered a severe restraint on the rights of men to do whatever they pleased with their property.[7] Thus, they should have a right to dispose of their property interests in slaves by setting them free.

*   *   *   *   *

Even before the Revolution, Virginia's approach to private manumissions had been secularly challenged. Civil justice concerns about keeping humans in bondage were added to the voices of religious groups after the War. In 1767, perhaps in response to the debacle over the Stamp Act, an article was published in the Virginia Gazette that began with: "Long and serious reflections upon the nature and consequences of slavery, . . . now, as freedom is unquestionably the birth-right of all mankind, Africans as well as Europeans, to keep the former in a state of slavery is a constant violation of the right and therefore justice."[8]

According to Professor Russell, the secular drive to permit manumission was proposed by a "younger set of men, who represented the liberal ideas of the English and French thought of that time, and prominent among them was Thomas Jefferson."[9] This drive began in 1769 when, as a member of the legislature, Thomas Jefferson seconded a motion to remove the restrictions on voluntary manumission.[10]

As in other parts of the country, Virginian Quakers, who had been slave owners up to the Revolutionary War, sought to convince others of the evil of the practice of slavery and its "inconsistency with [their] Christian profession."[11] Some petitioners argued to the Virginia legislature, "The glorious and ever memorable Revolution . . . can be justified on no other principles, but what do plead with still greater force for the emancipation of our slaves in proportion as the oppression exercised over them exceeds the oppression formerly exercised over the United States by Great Britain."[12]

When the Virginia legislature finally passed its Act to authorize the manumission of slaves in May, 1782, Professor Russell opined that men like Thomas Jefferson were "due much of the credit."[13] Virginia's Chapter XXI provided, "It is lawful for any person by last will and testament or other instrument in writing sealed and witnessed to emancipate and set free his slave or slaves. All slaves so set free, not being of sound mind and body, or being above forty-five years of age, or males under twenty-one and females under eighteen shall be supported by the persons liberating them."[14] Later that year, Chapter 41 slightly modified this rule by requiring, "Slaves may be emancipated by an instrument in writing, attested and proved by two witnesses; provided they shall be liable to be taken on execution to satisfy any debt contracted previously by the person so emancipating."[15] By requiring witnesses to a written instrument of manumission, Virginia put documents of manumission on par with deeds and other legal documents. The latter modification permitting creditors to take slaves to satisfy debts assisted in diminishing Thomas Jefferson's final estate to a negative value, meaning its obligations exceeded its assets.

After the passage of its 1782 Act permitting private manumissions, the Virginia legislature became even more generous toward permitting public emancipation. In 1783, they expressed gratitude to every black who fought or served as a freeman in the late war by pledging "the utmost protection of the State in the enjoyment of the freedom he had helped to gain."[16] Some slaves who served in the Revolutionary War were also set free, at legislative expense by paying their masters from the public treasury.[17] Professor Russell details several incidents where the Virginia legislature freed people for meritorious service in the Revolutionary War, for example.[18] Virginia essentially took the position that if it had the power to make a slave, it also possessed the power to "unmake a slave."[19]

With a measure of generosity of spirit, the Virginia legislature also validated wills that purported to free slaves before 1782. For example in 1777, a special legislative act manumitted Rachel and her child, the slaves of John Barr, in Northumberland County and confirmed his right to give them the sole use of certain property.[20] Nevertheless, in freeing these two individuals, the legislature specified that their actions should establish no precedent.[21] Thus, the legislature reserved the right to consider such wills on a case by case basis.

Russell opined, "This period from 1782 to 1806 was the time when manumission was most popular in Virginia, and is unique in the history of slavery in the State as being the only period when manumission went on at a rapid rate without legal restraint."[22] Courts also wrestled with the concept of private manumission by will or deed. One judge said that by freeing a slave, the master was not gifting the person property, but rather manumission "is the exoneration of a human being from the bonds which our institutions have fastened upon him."[23] This was in keeping with the proposition that slaves could not own property.

Privately, people manumitted slaves during their lives by deeds, or after their death in their last will and testament.[24] Professor Russell estimated that there were less than 3,000 Free Blacks in Virginia when the restraint on private manumission was removed in 1782, but within eight years, the population quadrupled to 12,886.[25] As an example, Russell cited William Binford and Robert Pleasants, of Henrico County, who respectively manumitted twelve and ninety slaves in 1782.[26]

The repeal of the Virginia's law against private manumissions led to freedom for the author's paternal ancestor, Gideon Hill. Benjamin Crawley, a Methodist minister, signed a deed in January 1787 freeing fifty slaves at once. The document began with the words, "Know all men by these presents that I Benjamin Crawley of Amelia County in the state of Virginia by virtue of the Act of Assembly in that ease made and provided do hereby emansipate [sic] and set free from bondage the following slaves or servants . . ."[27] The list included "Geddy aged two."[28] The timing of Mr. Crawley's emancipation deed followed by five years the act of Virginia permitting such emancipations after they had been severely restricted starting in 1782, which had proclaimed, "It is lawful for any person by last will and testament or other instrument in writing sealed and witnessed to emancipate and set free his slave or slaves."[29]

Crawley may have told Gideon's parents and several other relatives the previous December that their Christmas gift was their impending freedom. Minors, like Geddy (Gideon) could only be released from bondage if there was an adult simultaneously freed to become responsible for the person. Thus, when the first United States census was taken in 1790, these ancestors of the author were among the 12,866 Free Blacks in Virginia. Because Geddy was under the age of majority, Benjamin Crawley remained responsible for his care, and his family continued to live on the Crawley plantation.

Benjamin Crawley had been born in 1760 to Elizabeth and William Crawley in Amelia County, which had been formed in 1734 and named after Princess Amelia Sophia, the second daughter of George II. William Crawley, one of the largest landowners in Amelia County,[30] had received land patent rights to 3,714 acres in 1737 and 3,000 acres in 1750.[31] During the decade or so prior to the Revolutionary War outbreak, William served as an Amelia County Justice of the Peace and as a sheriff.[32]

Both William and Benjamin Crawley, supported the Revolutionary War effort. The *Virginia Publick Claims* book for Amelia County indicates that William gave up four "beeves," or cows, during one August valued at 17 Pounds and the Virginia militia borrowed waggonage from his estate the following January, which was valued at seven Pounds.[33] Benjamin Crawley contributed five "beeves," or cows, during one September valued at 28 pounds.[34] These were among the highest values for contributions to the war effort listed in the book. Many landowners contributed only one beef worth about two or three pounds.[35]

Meanwhile, Benjamin's older sister, Catherine Crawley Ward, got in a scuffle with British army officer Banastre Tarleton, whose personal motto for the joust was "swift, vigilant, and bold" and "reliance on shock and terror would make his name a byword for terror in the south."[36] Fearing a Tarleton raid while her husband Captain Benjamin Ward was defending Petersburg, Catherine left Amelia County with her son and valuables in a carriage only to encounter Tarleton's men in Burkeville where they made off with her "silks on the points of their swords."[37]

Catherine had good reason to fear Tarleton and his dragoons. During Revolutionary War skirmishes in Virginia, they captured seven members of the state legislature, including Daniel Boone, and laid waste to Thomas Jefferson's property at Elk Hill by burning his buildings and crops, eating up all his cows, sheep and hogs, and riding off on his horses.[38] In addition to Captain Benjamin Ward, who died in 1783, Catherine Crawley also married Daniel Jones, who served as an officer under Ward, and William Fitzgerald, who likewise served as an officer in the Revolutionary War.[39] Since all three men predeceased her, Catherine was a three-time Revolutionary War widow.

On one side of Amelia County's Deep Creek, Benjamin Crawley owned 1,652 acres of land and on the other side he possessed 1,200 acres.[40] He did not free all his slaves following the conclusion of the Revolutionary War. In contrast to his deed of emancipation in 1787, Benjamin Crawley's last will and testament bequeathed fifteen slaves and devised half of the "land lying on the west side of Deep Creek" to his nephew David Crawley Jones.[41] His will specified that all of these Negroes and the Deep Creek land had been given to him in his late brother John Crawley's last will and testament.[42] Benjamin was most likely the caretaker of his brother John's property until David came of age and could lawfully take possession of his own land and slaves. Benjamin devised the other half of the land on the west side of Deep Creek to his nephew Peter Robinson, who sold the acreage to William Old in 1795 Peter also became one of Benjamin's executors when his will was probated.

Since he did not free all of his slaves, what motivated Benjamin Crawley to free 50 slaves at once in 1787? Besides religious concerns about holding humans in bondage, perhaps a hint to the answer can be found in an April 24, 1792, deed that emancipated two more slaves, "a mulatto woman named Suckey, age 28, and her son Jonathan, age three months."[43] In keeping with the legal requirement to have witnesses to a deed of manumission, the attesting witnesses were William Old, Robert Chappel, and Abner Chappel.[44] A year later, Abner Chappel emancipated two of his slaves: Matt on

February 28, 1793, and Patram on April 25, 1793.[45] There were no witnesses to Chappel's deeds of emancipation, indicating that the requirement may have been haphazardly enforced.

Further information about Benjamin Crawley's relationship to Suckey can be found in his last will and testament, where pertinent clauses concern Suckey and her son Jonathan. Benjamin had purchased Suckey from John Jones, who was the brother of his sister Catherine's second husband, Daniel Jones. Benjamin left Suckey and Jonathan the residue of his estate, including all the land and personal property that he had not given to others. When some of Benjamin's executors did not honor the will's provisions and give Suckey the property left to her in his will, she successfully sued to enforce her legal rights. On January 22, 1801, Suckey was officially deeded the property left to her in the Last Will of Benjamin Crawley.[46]

There is also some indication that Benjamin Crawley may have married Suckey and legitimized Jonathan as his biological son. By the time of the 1810 census, Suckey had Anglicized her name to Susanna and adopted the surname Crawley.[47] She was listed as living in a household that included two free persons (herself and Jonathan) and seven slaves.[48] Since Suckey and Jonathan were recorded in the category of "persons not taxed," Amelia Country records assessed them according to the status of a white woman and a minor white male, two categories of the non-taxed.

Peter Robinson, Benjamin's nephew, was twice appointed Jonathan's guardian on February 25, 1797,[49] and in April 1799.[50] The appointment stated, "Peter Robinson Guardian of Jonathan orphan of Ben Crawley."[51] While legally Jonathan was born a slave and became a Free Black when Benjamin Crawley manumitted him, he was treated as the son of a white planter after his father's death.

Benjamin Crawley's actions toward Suckey and Jonathan contrasts dramatically when juxtaposed against Thomas Jefferson's actions toward Sally Hemings and their children. First, Benjamin freed Suckey and Jonathan in a deed of manumission during his lifetime. Jefferson, by comparison, permitted two of Sally's children,

Beverly and Harriet, to "run away" and manumitted the youngest sons, Eston and Madison, in the codicil to his will.

After his death, Sally was granted "her time" to go live with her children in Charlottesville, where she remained until her death in 1835. Benjamin Crawley directly secured Suckey and Jonathan's freedom, whereas Jefferson indirectly freed Sally and two of their children.

Second, by marrying Suckey, Benjamin Crawley legitimized Jonathan. Both took the Crawley surname after his death. Sally and all of her children remained Hemingses. After Eston and Madison left Virginia for Ohio following their mother's death, they did not change their surname to connect them to the Third President of the United States. Indeed, Madison acknowledged in a memoir published in 1873 that it was only after Jefferson's death he learned about his father's public life.[52]

Third, Benjamin Crawley financed Suckey and Jonathan's lives following his death by gifting them a considerable landed estate. The bulk of Jefferson's belongings, including Monticello and most of his slaves, were sold to satisfy his debts. His family of color did not receive anything to live on.

Even though Jefferson appeared to have done so little to acknowledge and support his family of color, Jefferson perhaps proved he loved Sally, whom his grandson Thomas Jefferson Randolph described as "light colored and decidedly good looking,"[53] because he honored his commitment made in Paris to free all of her children should she return with him to Monticello. At the time, countless other planters were selling off their children by enslaved women.

Unlike many male historians who denied that a relationship had even existed between Sally Hemings and Thomas Jefferson, modern female historians[54] analyzed the documentary evidence and presented the case that a love relationship existed between them that lasted over several decades, beginning when he was ambassador to Paris and continuing through his presidency, his retirement from public life, and his return to Monticello. The relationship was well known in Virginia and little discussed until Jefferson became president. It became the subject of scandal when James Callender, a journalist, "made the first public allegation that Jefferson had been involved in a sexual relationship with Sally Hemings."[55]

*   *   *   *   *

Benjamin Crawley and Thomas Jefferson's actions in creating families of color were illegal. After the Revolutionary War, Virginia legislators continued to write statutes punishing both adultery and miscegenation. In 1792, the Virginia legislature passed Chapter 72 to provide that "[e]very person . . . committing adultery or fornication, . . . shall forfeit $20.00 for adultery and $10.00 for fornication" if convicted.[56] And then there was Chapter 42, which was enacted to prevent white men and white women from intermarrying with Negroes or mulattoes.[57] "Those who married could be imprisoned for six months, and ordered to pay $30.00, and a minister who married Negroes and whites was fined $250 for each such marriage."[58] Neither Crawley nor Jefferson was ever indicted, convicted, or paid fines for consummating their relationships with Suckey and Sally. Nor did Crawley go to prison for marrying Suckey. While Virginia legislators may not have wanted couples to engage in interracial sex and marry the objects of their desire, they did not actively enforce their statutes.

Crawley and Jefferson's examples confirm that whites persisted in intermingling with mulattos and producing mixed-race children into the second, third, and fourth generations, some of whom eventually passed into white society. In 1785, the Virginia legislature defined a mulatto as a person possessing one-fourth or more Negro blood.[59] Those with less than one-fourth Negro blood who, for example, only had a great-grandparent who was half or full Negro were presumed to be white by this time.[60] Sally Hemings, who was three-quarter's white and described as "mighty near white" by former Monticello slave Isaac Granger Jefferson,[61] was still defined as a Negro, but her children by Jefferson should have been defined as white. However, they were born to her, an enslaved woman, which made her progeny slaves. Super light-skinned people were sometimes referred to as "white slaves." The Comte de Volney, a French man visiting Monticello in 1796, observed that Jefferson owned slaves "as white as I am."[62]

By running away to Washington City or to Philadelphia, Sally Hemings' oldest children, Beverley and Harriet, passed into white society and became "free white citizen[s] of the United States."[63] In his memoir, Madison said that Beverly went to Washington as a white man, married a white woman in Maryland, and had a daughter.[64] Their sister Harriet assumed the role of a white woman, married a white man in good standing, and raised a family of children in Washington City, according to Madison.[65]

After being freed in Jefferson's will,[66] Eston and Madison became Free Blacks. According to Madison, his brother Eston married a colored woman in Virginia, moved first to Ohio and second to Wisconsin where he died leaving three children.[67] Madison married a Free Black woman in Virginia, where they remained until 1836 before moving to Ohio. He and his wife Mary McCoy had nine children, one of whom died during the Civil War at the Anderson prison pen.[68]

Like Beverly and Harriet Hemings, Jonathan Crawley also passed into white society after having been born a mulatto slave, but his path was different. Jonathan later sold all of his Virginia property, including 900 of the acres inherited from his father Benjamin, to his cousin David C. Jones in 1816, and migrated to Missouri. The Missouri Compromise permitted Missouri's admission as a slave state in 1821 following Maine's admission as a free state in 1820 to keep the balance between free and slave states.

In Missouri, unlike in Amelia County, Virginia, where everyone knew that his mother was a mulatto, Jonathan was able to pass into white society, free of the burdens connected to Negro blood. The second census taken while Jonathan was living in Missouri designated him as white. His son, Benjamin Franklin Crawley, graduated from Yale College in 1847 and became a school teacher in Missouri.[69] One-hundred and thirty-eight years later, Gideon Hill's fourth great-granddaughter, Sherri Burr, graduated from Yale Law School and became a university professor.

The comparative stories of Benjamin Crawley and Thomas Jefferson's children illustrate the privileges associated with social status. When born slaves, their children possessed no legal rights. When they became Free Blacks, they received partial rights. When they passed into white society, they were accorded all advantages connected to white skin.

By statute, the Virginia Legislature sometimes proclaimed a person to be white, and it could have done so with Jefferson's children and Crawley's child, but no such application was ever made. An 1833 statute specifically declared that parties named Wharton were "not Negroes or mulattoes but white persons, although remotely descended from a colored woman."[70] The Whartons, for example, had previously been held in slavery but had acquired their freedom in 1806.[71] The Whartons thus migrated in status from "white slaves" to just white.

The success of the Revolutionary War and the creation of the United States of America brought freedom for white men, and some of the enslaved who became Free Blacks either through public emancipations or private manumissions. As Jefferson was creating his family of color, which he did not acknowledge, he was also rising in public esteem. He became one of four of the first five presidents to hail from the Old Dominion. All of these men contributed to the ongoing national discussion about slavery and its evils, and interacted with Free Blacks. Jefferson's actions in these matters contrasted distinctly with other national leaders.

NINE

*

The Anti-Slavery
Slaveholding Paradox

Twelve of the first eighteen United States presidents owned slaves at some point during their lifetimes. The six who never owned humans as property included John Adams, John Quincy Adams, Millard Fillmore, Franklin Pierce, James Buchanan, and Abraham Lincoln. Virginia gifted the nation four of its first five presidents, all of whom enslaved multiple people. Although Thomas Jefferson often railed against the institution of slavery, he benefited from his ownership of as many as 1,000 slaves over the course of his lifetime, substantially more than any other president. Several of the slave-holding leaders interacted with Free Blacks, either professionally, in war, as lawyers, through correspondence, or in their personal lives. And, of course, some were known to engage in intimate relations with persons of African descent.

This chapter contrasts the actions toward blacks, both the free and enslaved, of Thomas Jefferson with those of four northern national leaders who also owned slaves (Benjamin Franklin, Aaron Burr, Alexander Hamilton, and John Jay) and with three of Virginia's other slaveholding presidents (George Washington, James Madison, and James Monroe). These leaders lived lives of constant conflict between what they said about the entitlement of blacks to liberty and their ownership of human property. All of them declared slavery as evil, an abomination, or an institution that should be abolished. All the Virginians died leaving estates containing slaves, while the northerners had divested themselves of human capital before their demise. Jefferson stands out among these leaders because he wrote the most contradictory words against slavery and took some steps to end it, while holding the largest number of men, women, and children in bondage.

In the incongruity between their thoughts and actions, the third United States president and other national leaders exemplified living with contradictions. According to F. Scott Fitzgerald, "The test of a first-rate intelligence is the ability to hold two opposed ideas in mind at the same time and still retain the ability to function."[1]

Jefferson demonstrated this ability to function in two diametrically opposed universes through his writings that contained bifurcating thoughts. He wrote, "All men are created equal" in the Declaration of Independence and a diatribe about how blacks were inferior to whites in his only published book, *Notes on the State of Virginia*. He criticized the "eternal monotony" of African skin that failed to show blushes, and indicated that he had never heard a black utter a thought above the plain level of narration or produce art such as paintings and sculpture.[2] As he aged among his slaves, Jefferson had opportunities to observe that black skin possessed a beneficial quality in that it tended to wrinkle less than white skin, but he never wrote another book to correct his initial observation.

His paternalist approach to those he held in bondage is evident in this sentence he wrote to Edward Bancroft on January 26, 1789, "To give liberty to, or rather to abandon persons whose habits have been formed in slavery is like abandoning children."[3]

Through interactions with his slaves who learned to read and write, Jefferson could have observed that the condition of slavery was not conducive to pursuing creative and educational endeavors. Despite legal bans prohibiting masters from educating their slaves and slaves from educating each other,[4] many overcame the chains intended to shortchange their brains. Indeed, "[a] number of Jefferson's slaves could read *and* write," including Madison Hemings, Peter Fossett, John Hemings, and James Hemings.[5] Jefferson's white grandchildren taught the "ABCs" to Madison and Peter.[6]

Moreover, the word "Doublethink" applies to what Jefferson said and wrote about Free Blacks. George Orwell fashioned the word in his book *Nineteen Eighty-Four* as an explanation for the acts of ordinary people simultaneously accepting two mutually contradictory beliefs as correct, often in distinct social contexts, such as speaking out against slavery while owning slaves. Doublethink is notable because "the person is completely unaware of any conflict or contradiction."[7] Burr, however, saw the conflict clearly and acted to correct it.

Jefferson's own words support the view that he engaged in doublethink about slavery's blows to its victims his entire life. In 1786, he described American enslavement as "a bondage, one hour of which is fraught with more misery" than the tyranny the American revolutionaries had revolted against. In 1814, twelve years before he died on the 50th anniversary of the Declaration of Independence, Jefferson said that American slaves are better fed, warmer clothed, "and labor less than the journeymen or day-laborers of England," and they live "without want, or fear of it."[8]

In the first quotation, the Sage of Monticello may have been thinking of his field hands and in the latter about his house slaves, such as the Hemingses of Monticello. House slaves, like the Hemingses, were granted special privileges, and many probably lived lives "without want, or fear of it." Field hands, however, labored from sunup to sundown, and those who had the misfortune to be sold to labor camps in Louisiana and Mississippi suffered torture as their masters pushed them to increase their productivity.[9]

Indeed their misery appears similar to that endured by slaves in Portuguese Brazil, Spanish Veracruz, and on the Caribbean sugar islands. Nevertheless, if Jefferson had polled both sets of bonded groups on his plantation and asked whether they preferred liberty over slavery, they would have, no doubt, opted for liberty. In the rare instances when Virginia's blacks had a choice between enslavement and liberty and chose the former, they did so primarily to be near their families who remained enslaved. Sally Hemings may have in part been motivated to return from Paris, where she was free, to Monticello, where she would be re-enslaved, to be near her mother and other family members.

Jefferson also demonstrated cognitive dissonance towards blacks is his *Notes on the State of Virginia*. This psychological term has been defined as "the mental stress or discomfort experienced by an individual who holds two or more contradictory beliefs, ideas, or values at the same time, performs an action that is contradictory to one or more beliefs, ideas or values."[10]

In five of the book's pages, Jefferson revealed that "he found almost every aspect of Africans inferior. . . [including their] kinky hair."[11] He also felt that blacks were less physically attractive. Yet, his longest intimate relationship was with Sally Hemings, his concubine who was one-quarter African. The "decidedly good looking"[12] Sally apparently did not possess kinky hair since she was described as "having long straight hair down her back."[13] She may even have favored Jefferson's deceased wife Martha, who shared a father with Sally Hemings.

Perhaps in Jefferson's mind he excused his relationship with Sally Hemings because she was a mulatto who was three-quarters white and one-quarter African[14] and their children would be considered white since they were only one-eighth Negro.[15] Jefferson had opined that once someone possessed only one-eighth Negro blood, or "three crossings" with whites, they should be considered white.[16] Maybe he did love her, and suffered no mental stress from writing negatively about people of African descent while having a physical relationship with one. Certainly, for his image, it was better for Jefferson's reputation to have adored Sally and formed a consensual relationship with her than for him to have engaged in the master rape of a teenager.

Despite the racist thoughts expressed in print, Jefferson feared the section he wrote on why slavery should end could become his more criticized section. In drafting the Declaration of Independence, Jefferson blamed King George III for the slave trade. Of all the founding fathers and national leaders, Jefferson harangued passionately against slavery while benefitting extensively from the humans who were forced to labor for his happiness.[17] As such, his words, thoughts, and actions toward Free Blacks and the enslaved must be compared to other anti-slavery slaveholders in both the North and the South.

* * * * *

The Northern Anti-Slavery Slaveholders

Among the famous northern slaveholders was founding father Benjamin Franklin, a Pennsylvanian who was born in Boston on January 17, 1706.[18] Franklin's professional life began as an indentured servant, similar to many of the Africans who arrived on the shores of Virginia from 1619 to 1670. Josiah Franklin induced his son Benjamin to sign indenture papers that committed him to work for his older brother James as a printing apprentice.[19]

In his autobiography, Benjamin Franklin wrote about James, "Though a brother, he considered himself as my master . . . and had often beaten me."[20] Unlike Anthony Johnson, the Free Black who finished his indentured service before going into business for himself as a planter, Benjamin Franklin fled from his indenture servitude with three years remaining on his contract.[21] He was seventeen. Unlike John Punch, who was punished for running away by having his indentured service for a term of years transformed into service for life, Benjamin Franklin's flight led to riches, adventure, and Founding Fatherhood.

Different from Jefferson who was born into a slaveholding family, Benjamin Franklin became a slaveholder in adulthood. In 1751, when he was forty-five, Franklin sold a slave couple that he owned because "he did not like having 'Negro servants,' and he found them uneconomical."[22] Similar to Jefferson in *Notes on the State of Virginia*, Franklin wrote racist remarks about blacks while attacking

slavery, indicating a certain dissonance in his thinking. In Franklin's
"Observations on the Increase of Mankind," he commented about
"almost every slave being by nature a thief" while writing that slavery negatively diminishes a nation because it makes no economic
sense and causes white children to become proud and disgusted
with labor.[23]

Evidence also endures that he "personally traded in slaves, buy-
ing and selling from his Market Street print shop."[24] In his newspaper, flyers advertised "A likely Negro woman to be sold" and "a likely
young Negro fellow," and ended with instructions on how to purchase the individual.[25] The enslaved Africans who were mentioned
in Franklin's correspondence included Peter, Jemima, Othello (who
died young), King, and George. The latter two were kept as personal
servants, despite Franklin having written, "Slavery is such an atro-
cious debasement of human nature."[26]

While Franklin was serving his country on a diplomatic mission
in Europe, one of his slaves ran away and did not return. In his later
years, Franklin became an ardent abolitionist as president of the
Society for Promoting the Abolition of Slavery and the Relief of Negroes Unlawfully Held in Bondage in 1775.[27] This group published
a plan for the education of former slaves "To instruct, to advise, to
qualify those who have been restored to freedom, for the exercise
and enjoyment of civil liberty."[28] The plan also promised "to furnish
them with employment suited to their age, sex, talents, and other
circumstances; and to promote their children an education calculated for their future situation in life."[29]

The Pennsylvania Abolition Society still exists, and considers itself to have been the first abolition society in the world. Its current
mission confronts racism, preserves African American monuments,
provides scholarships for persons of African American descent, and
improves the quality of race relations in Pennsylvania.

Perhaps Franklin's conversion from slaveholder to abolitionist in
the final quarter of his life was motivated by his turn as an indentured servant during the first quarter of his life. Like Captain John
Smith who had been enslaved in Turkey before voyaging to Virginia

and who argued against the custom based on experience, Franklin was forced to work for someone against his will. By contrast, Thomas Jefferson had been fed with silver forks by slaves all his life, and never experienced the toll that forced servitude inflicted on the minds, spirits, and bodies of the enslaved.

Franklin's final will stipulated that his son-in-law, Richard Bache, should not receive his inheritance unless he freed his slave, Bob.[30] Bache honored Franklin's requirement, whose 1757 will also decreed that "my Negro Man Peter, and his Wife Jemima, be free after my Decease," but they died before Franklin. By comparison, the codicil to Jefferson's will freed only men related to his concubine, or substitute wife, Sally Hemings. At 11:00 p.m. on April 17, 1790, when Benjamin Franklin passed on to that "Great Mystery in the Sky,"[31] he owned no slaves. Thus, at the end of his life, Franklin's actions regarding slavery aligned with his thoughts and writings.

* * * * *

Prominent New Yorkers Aaron Burr, Alexander Hamilton, and John Jay were all anti-slavery slaveholders who became members of the New York Manumission Society.[32] Like Jefferson, all of them were capable lawyers who transitioned into public service.

While many esteemed members of the Society owned slaves, Burr "appears to have viewed slavery as a temporary condition of servitude rather than a status based on racial inferiority."[33] In their professional lives, Burr and Jefferson both represented mulattos. As a lawyer, Burr represented two manumitted brothers who sued for their portion of their white slaveholder-father's estate.[34] During Jefferson's approximately eight-year legal career from 1767 to 1774, he sued on behalf of mixed-raced Samuel Howell who sought freedom from indentured servitude. When Jefferson lost the case, he gave Howell money, which the latter used for self-liberation and ran away.[35]

Both Burr and Jefferson oversaw their daughters' education, but differed in their views on the education of blacks. Theodosia Burr was introduced to a rigorous curriculum early in life, and could read and write by the time she was three. As he did with his daughter,

Theodosia, Aaron Burr ensured that his slaves were educated. He insisted that his house slaves Tom learn to read and write and Carlos learn to play the violin.[36] In a letter to his daughter, Burr was shocked that a friend of his had "mocked the idea that Carlos might learn to play the violin."[37] In contrast, while Jefferson made sure both Patsy and Polly received an education in Paris, he was overheard telling the Marquis de Lafayette that slaves should only be taught to read, but not to write, as that would "enable them to forge papers, when they could no longer be kept in subjugation."[38]

Burr and Jefferson were among the men who received Electoral College votes in the 1796 presidential election. While John Adams was elected president with 71 votes, Thomas Jefferson was elected vice-president with 68 votes, and Burr came in fourth with 30 votes.[39] In the election of 1800 (the country's third), Burr and Jefferson tied in the Electoral College after Jefferson defeated John Adams in the popular vote. At the time, electors did not distinguish between president and vice president, but rather the highest vote obtainer won the presidency and the second highest won the vice-presidency. Because Jefferson and Burr both won 73 electoral votes, the election was thrown to the House of Representatives. After thirty-six ballots and the intervention of Alexander Hamilton to support Jefferson, the primary author of the Declaration of Independence became the nation's third president and Burr was elected its third vice-president.

As the third vice-president of the United States, Aaron Burr shared something personal in common with the third president, Thomas Jefferson. Both were sworn into the nation's highest offices having already created families with women of color.[40] The Aaron Burr Association confirmed that family oral and recorded history "in combination with a plethora of circumstantial evidence builds a convincing case for substantiating the existence of Aaron Burr's second family."[41]

In 1788, Burr's daughter Louisa Charlotte Burr was born to Mary Eugénie Beauharnais Emmons, a servant in Burr's Philadelphia household. Emmons was reportedly from Calcutta, India, but had lived in the West Indies before migrating to the United States. Emmons also gave birth to a son, John "Jean" Pierre Burr, on August 26, 1792, while traveling between Haiti and Pennsylvania.[42]

Although John Pierre Burr was sometimes referred to as Aaron Burr's "illegitimate son" or "natural son" during his lifetime, according to Harvard historian Allen Ballard, Aaron Burr married Mary Emmons following the death of his wife Theodosia.[43] Ballard, who is a third great-grandson of John Pierre Burr and fourth great-grandson of Aaron Burr, states that his great aunt, Elizabeth (Doll) Durham, witnessed the destruction of the marriage certificate.[44] Such a marriage would have legitimized both John Pierre and Louisa Charlotte Burr.

Unlike three of Jefferson's children of color who married into white society, Louisa Charlotte and John Pierre Burr both married Free Blacks in Pennsylvania. Louisa Charlotte married Francis Webb, a founding member of the Pennsylvania Augustine Education Society. Their son, Frank J. Webb, wrote the second published novel, *The Garies and Their Friends*, by an African American author, in 1857. The novel contained a preface signed by Harriet Beecher Stowe, the author of Uncle Tom's Cabin. She wrote that "the incidents related are mostly true ones, woven together by a slight web of fiction."[45]

John Pierre Burr married Hetty Elizabeth Emery, the daughter of John Emery. As a Free Black, John Emery served as a private in Pennsylvania's Fifth Regiment, which was commanded by Colonel Francis Johnston, during the Revolutionary War.[46]

John Pierre Burr became a barber to white men and a conductor on the Underground Railroad.[47] He and his wife hid fugitive slaves in their Philadelphia home at Fifth and Locust (then Prune) streets in the attic, a cave in the cellar, and a deep hole in the backyard.[48] John Emery Burr, John Pierre and Hetty's oldest son, was often told by his parents to ignore the noises in the cellar or attic.[49] The runaways remained in the Burr home until John Pierre could safely transport them at night to their next conductor who would see them safely to a meeting with Lucretia Mott, a Quaker, and onwards to Canada.

John Pierre Burr also became an organizer of the Pennsylvania Anti-Slavery Society and served as an agent for William Lloyd Garrison's abolitionist newspaper, *The Liberator*.[50] In political life, John Pierre Burr protested the disenfranchisement of Free Blacks by the Pennsylvania state legislature in 1838. As such, he ardently practiced the anti-slavery beliefs that he shared with his father, Aaron Burr.

Different from Jefferson, Aaron Burr did not enslave his children or their mother. Both Louisa Charlotte and John Pierre took Burr's last name, and he communicated with them throughout their lives.

Jefferson and Burr created plans to eliminate slavery. As discussed earlier, Burr sought the immediate emancipation of New York slaves and voted against bills that restricted the rights of Free Blacks. Jefferson wanted to mandate that all children born of slave parents after 1800 be set free after attaining adulthood, and trained as apprentices who could then be deported from the state.[51] As president, Jefferson did obtain a bill ending the transatlantic importation of slaves to the United States after January 1, 1808. One historian deemed this as "perhaps Jefferson's most influential act against slavery."[52]

Burr's relationship with Jefferson, and his political influence, deteriorated after his duel with Alexander Hamilton in Weehawken, New Jersey, in 1804. Following the conclusion of his vice-presidency, Burr migrated west with plans to create an independent state, which led to Jefferson having him tried twice for treason.[53] With his acquittals in the rear view of a ship's stern, Burr crossed the Atlantic Ocean and lived in Paris between 1810 and 1811, something Jefferson had done between 1785 and 1789.

✻　✻　✻　✻　✻

Twenty-four years before Alexander Hamilton succumbed to the deadly events that transpired in Weehawken, New Jersey in 1804, he married into the slaveholding family of Elizabeth "Eliza" Schuyler in 1780. Ron Chernow, Hamilton's acclaimed biographer, wrote, "three oblique hints in Hamilton's papers suggests that he and Eliza *may* have owned one or two household slaves."[54] One so-called hint came from Hamilton debiting his cashbook to pay his father-in-law

Philip Schuyler "for 2 Negro servants purchased by him for me."[55] Most people would consider this definite proof, and not a mere hint, that Hamilton was a slaveholder because he paid to purchase two human beings.

Reimbursing a father-in-law for two slaves, however, pales in comparison to Jefferson's hoards. In 1774 when he married Martha Wales Skelton, Jefferson already owned 52 slaves. He acquired an additional 135 slaves upon the death of John Wayles, Martha's father who was a lawyer and slave trader. The combination placed Jefferson "among the largest slaveholders in Virginia."[56]

Divergent from Jefferson who believed blacks were "innately inferior" to whites, Hamilton "expressed an unwavering belief in the genetic equality of blacks and whites."[57] Chernow wrote that Hamilton "was enlightened for his day," probably "from his personal boyhood experience"[58] living on the island of Nevis with enslaved and Free Blacks.

✳   ✳   ✳   ✳   ✳

John Jay, "a defender of liberty,"[59] served as governor of New York, President of the Continental Congress, and as the first chief justice of the United States. Jay also negotiated the Peace Treaty of 1783 that ended the Revolutionary War and the Jay Treaty of 1794 to protect commerce with Great Britain. He brought his slave Abby to France, and while he was visiting London in 1783, she ran away.[60] Accustomed to being obeyed, Jay was apparently surprised by Abby's act of self-liberation because he had promised to free her upon their return to the United States.[61] Unbeknownst to Abby, she could have claimed her freedom in France, as Sally and James Hemings considered doing while living in Paris with Jefferson a few years later.

When Abby was apprehended, she refused to accept release if she promised to "behave well, . . . saying she was very happy where she was for she had nothing to do."[62] Jay left her in jail for about twenty days, apparently at the suggestion of Benjamin Franklin, to teach her a lesson.[63] She contracted an illness while incarcerated and died within three weeks of returning to Jay.[64] The only person who perhaps learned a lesson from the incident was Jay. Too harsh of treatment toward human property can lead to having no human property.

In *John Jay: Founding Father*, Walter Stahr speculated that perhaps moved by Abby's death, Jay signed a "conditional manumission" of his slave Benoit, which he started with the statement "the children of men are by nature equally free, and cannot without justice be either reduced to or held in slavery."[65] The document demonstrated that Jay seemed completely unaware of any cognitive dissonance, conflict or contradiction, between his writing about freedom and his requiring Benoit to continue as a slave. Perhaps Jay wrote this document to give Benoit written proof of his intent to manumit him since his oral assurances to Abby had been in vain.

*   *   *   *   *

The Virginian Anti-Slavery Slaveholders

George Washington became a slave owner at age 11 when his father Augustine died and devised a 280-acre estate near Fredericksburg and bequeathed ten slaves to him. As a young adult, Washington first bought eight slaves and then more. A few years after he purchased Mount Vernon, Washington married Martha Dandridge Custis, one of the richest widows in Virginia, and acquired the labor of another 84 slaves.

Although Washington professed to prefer motivating slaves with encouragement and rewards, he sometimes approved of "corrections," or the infliction of harsh punishment on his slaves, including whipping and giving them taxing work assignments. Washington also disciplined the troops under his command harshly. As David McCullough wrote in the book *1776*, "He wanted rules and regulations adopted, punishments made more severe."[66] Without Washington's knowledge, Congress enacted "stiffer punishments for major offenses [from 39 to up to one hundred lashes], and increased the number of crimes for which the penalty was death."[67]

Indeed, like other planters of his generation, George Washington often referred to the humans that he kept in bondage as "this species of property." This was similar to how "he described his dogs and horses," according to historian Joseph Ellis.[68]

Perhaps because of the conditions they experienced at Mount Vernon before the War, several of Washington's slaves escaped from Mount Vernon during the war. Seventeen, for example, fled to the British warship *HMS Savage* anchored in the Potomac off the shore of the plantation.[69] Washington also sold slaves who were recaptured[70] to the West Indies where they most likely never saw their families again.

From the President's house in Philadelphia, Ona Judge, who was Martha's personal maid, ran off. George and Martha Washington relentlessly pursued her as a fugitive. As historian Erica Armstrong Dunbar recounts in the gripping tale, *Never Caught*,[71] their efforts were inept because Ona Judge added herself to the Free Black population.

Jefferson was known to prefer humane treatment of slaves. There is no record that he ever personally whipped anyone. He also "demanded minimum physical discipline and, when away from Monticello, always cautioned his overseers against harsh treatment."[72] Jefferson believed that "well-treated slaves were more productive."[73] His white grandson, Thomas Jefferson (Jeff) Randolph, was known to delight in personally whipping slaves.[74]

He, did, however, sell and have Hubbard, a chronic runaway from Monticello, whipped in front of other slaves when he was recaptured to discourage others from deciding to self-liberate from bondage.[75] Jefferson suggested to the purchaser of Hubbard that he sell him because "the course he has been in and all the circumstances convince me he will never serve any man as a slave."[76] In his dealings with Hubbard, Jefferson revealed his true slaver instincts to punish and sell those who will not submit to his mastery of them.

Washington and Jefferson both had professional encounters with blacks. Washington's contacts with free black soldiers during the

Revolutionary War may have changed his attitudes toward slavery. He began to speak of the institution as the "only unavoidable subject of regret" of his public life. He wrote to Robert Morris, "There is not a man living . . . who wishes more sincerely than I do, to see a plan adopted for the gradual abolition of it."[77] He also expressed his "wishes to see some plan adopted by which slavery may be abolished by law."[78]

Poet Phyllis Wheatley dedicated a poem to Washington in 1775 to commemorate his appointment to lead the Continental Army. It contained the following verses:

> *Proceed, great chief, with virtue on thy side,*
> *Thy ev'ry action let the goddess guide.*
> *A crown, a mansion, and a throne that shine,*
> *With gold unfading, Washington! Be thine.*[79]

Washington politely responded to her poem and addressed her as "Miss Phillis." He wrote, "I thank you most sincerely for your polite notice of me, . . . and however undeserving I may be . . . the style and manner exhibit a striking proof of your great poetical Talents." He concluded his letter by saying that should Wheatley ever come to Cambridge he would be "happy to see a person so favored by the muses."[80] This was, according to the Mount Vernon website, Washington's only known correspondence with an enslaved person.[81]

Unlike Washington's gracious correspondence with Wheatley, Jefferson's interactions with Benjamin Banneker, who had been born free in Baltimore, could be subjected to multiple interpretations. Banneker demonstrated skills as a mathematician and an astronomer in his almanac. He sent a copy to Jefferson, who forwarded Banneker's almanac to the Marquis De Condorcet, secretary of the Academy of Sciences in Paris, and described Banneker as "a very respectable Mathematician." Later, however, Jefferson slighted Banneker by questioning whether he had received the aid of his neighbor in producing his book,[82] implying that if the book was excellent it could not have been written only by a black person.

Gordon-Reed proffered that the "self-protective" Jefferson's divergent writings on Banneker may have been a response to the criticism he received in the Federalist Press.[83] Possibly, Jefferson may have just been unaware of any inconsistency in the manner in which he interacted with this Free Black.

Like Washington, who observed the courage of Free Black soldiers during the Revolutionary War and wrote positively about their service to the Continental Congress, asking that Free Blacks be permitted to reenlist, Jefferson also wrote something positive about blacks. "In music," he wrote "they are generally more gifted than the whites with accurate ears for tune and time."[84] This was, indeed, a compliment to black musicians because Jefferson, who played the violin and cello, had said that music was "the favorite passion of [his] soul."[85]

He might also have written that blacks were gifted with money because on several occasions Jefferson borrowed from Free Blacks and his slaves when he was short on funds. We know this because he meticulously recorded all his borrowing and repaying of money in his Farm Book. While Jefferson logged all of his expenses and income, along with other detailed records about plantation affairs at Monticello, in his Farm Book,[86] he never added up the two sides of the ledger. Perhaps, according to one historian, he did not understand double-entry booking.[87] Thus, he never tracked the extent of his indebtedness until it overwhelmed him.

Towards the end of his life, he proposed a lottery to provide income for his estate. He hoped the sale of the tickets would "pay my debts and leave a living for myself in my old age, and leave something for my family."[88] To the end, Jefferson exhibited financial illiteracy. The lottery idea fizzled and three years after his death, Monticello, the land, the furnishings, and Jefferson's human property were sold and dispersed, leaving his white family, for whom he felt responsible, destitute. His daughter Martha stayed with her children, other relatives, or in rented homes. As Lucia Standard aptly noted in '*Those Who Labor For My Happiness*,' the plantation "family" that Jefferson had nurtured and controlled for sixty years was no more.

In the end, he had abandoned his "children"[89] (inclusive of his white family and slaves) to his creditors.

Fortunately, Washington was a better steward of his personal finances than Jefferson. At the end of his life, he neither abandoned his married family, nor his slaves. When Washington died, there were 318 enslaved people living on Mount Vernon, of whom he owned 123. In his will, Washington wrote, "Upon the decease of my wife, it is my Will & desire that all the slaves which I hold in my own right, shall receive their freedom. . . . I do hereby expressly forbid the Sale, or transportation out of the said Commonwealth of any slave I may die possessed of, under any pretense whatsoever."[90]

Washington's slaves, however, did not have to wait until Martha's death to be liberated from bondage. Abigail Adams explained to her sister that Martha Washington "did not feel as though her Life was safe in their hands, many of whom would be told that it was [in] their interest to get rid of her. . . . She therefore was advised to set them all free at the close of the year."[91] Thus, motivated at least in part by self-interest, Martha Washington signed a deed of manumission in December 1800, which became effective in January 1801, to add 123 individuals to Virginia's population of Free Blacks.

Unlike Washington, Jefferson did not arrange for the freedom of all his slaves in his will. Rather, Jefferson arranged to only manumit five slaves, all of whom were connected to Sally Hemings. Curiously, he referred to their youngest sons, Eston and Madison, as the apprentices of John Hemings in his will.[92] Thus, even in his last legal act, he did not acknowledge his paternity of Sally Hemings' children.

* * * * *

Of all the Founding Fathers, the two named James—Madison and Monroe—were probably Jefferson's best friends. They would follow him to become governors of Virginia and presidents of the United States. The third, fourth, and fifth presidents owned plantations in Virginia, with Monroe's Ashland being closer than Madison's Montpelier to Jefferson's Monticello. Like Jefferson, Madison and

Monroe spoke out against slavery while maintaining their property rights in humans.

Madison had a prime role in the Constitutional Convention that led to him being called the "Father of the Constitution." Although he did not propose the Three-Fifths Compromise found in Article 1, Section 2, Clause 3 of the Constitution, Madison and all the slaveholding presidents benefitted from its passage. The clause read, "Representatives and direct Taxes shall be apportioned among the several States which may be included within this union, according to their respective Numbers, which shall be determined by adding to the whole Number of free Persons, including those bound to Service for a Term of Years, and excluding Indians not taxed, three fifths of all other Persons."[93]

Even though they had no right to vote, three-fifths of all the slaves were counted to increase the voting power of white landowning males who could vote. Although Free Blacks, women, and indentured servants lacked voting rights, they were counted as whole people for assessing voting power by the states. This clause led to Virginia dominating the Electoral College, and producing four out of the first five presidents. Further, more slaveholders, than non slaveholders, were elected as president during the first hundred years following the Declaration of Independence.

Madison freed no slaves during his lifetime or upon his death. He did sell his slave Billey to a Quaker after Billey had spent some time with him in Philadelphia. Madison wrote that Philadelphia's freewheeling style had "tainted" Billey's mind, implying that he was no longer fit for enslavement. By 1783, the Quakers had become avid abolitionists, and the sale likely led to Billey's freedom without Madison having to do it. His will left everything to his wife Dolley. Although born a Quaker, Dolley had been excommunicated when she married into Madison's slaveholding family. She also did not free any of her enslaved humans.

In the 1820 census, 15 whites and 106 slaves lived on Madison's Montpelier plantation. Madison's large investment in human capital did not stop him from writing to Francis Wright on September

1, 1825, "The magnitude of this evil among us is so deeply felt, and so universally acknowledged, that no merit could be greater than that of devising a satisfactory remedy for it."[94] Madison agreed with Jefferson that blacks should be colonized on another continent once they were granted their freedom. After he retired, he became president of the American Colonization Society.

Similarly, James Monroe freed none of his enslaved people during his lifetime nor in his will from further bondage on his Ashlawn plantation. He had written, "What was the origin of our slave population? The evil commenced when we were in our colonial state, but acts were passed by our colonial Legislature, prohibiting the importation of more slaves into the colony. . . . Virginia . . . did all that was in her power to do, to prevent the extension of slavery, and to mitigate its evils."[95] Monroe's solution was to further the work of the American Colonization Society and arrange for the resettlement of as many Free Blacks as possible on a continent far from their birth.

Monroe agreed with Jefferson that Blacks needed to be relocated after being manumitted because blacks and whites could not live together in peace and harmony. Monroe encouraged the resettlement of Free Blacks in Africa. A special census was taken asking Free Blacks if they would like to be relocated to Liberia, a country on the west coast of Africa with no connection to their historic homelands. The leaders of Liberia named their new capital Monrovia after James Monroe, a patron of the movement.

Jefferson shared the beliefs of his two friends that it was impossible for blacks and whites to live together in the United States, and that people of African origin should be shipped to another country. However, during his lifetime, Jefferson's actions indicated otherwise. Unlike Madison and Monroe, Jefferson freed six people either informally or by deed, and five in his will. By deed, Jefferson liberated James Hemings, his cook who returned from France with Jefferson, to teach another relative the art of French cookery. Martin and Robert Hemings also received manumissions from Jefferson during his lifetime.

Even though Jefferson felt Free Blacks should not be allowed to remain in Virginia following their manumission, the codicil to his will requested special dispensation from the Virginia legislature to allow Burwell Colbert, Joseph Fossett, John Hemings, and the two Hemings brothers to remain not just in America but in Virginia. About his final acts of manumission, Gordon-Reed wrote, "What Jefferson accomplished for his children, and some of their relatives, was just what he stated could not be accomplished in the nation as a whole."[96] She added, "As was often the case, the public rhetorical Jefferson was very different from the down-to-personal-business Jefferson, the one he seldom wanted anyone to see."[97]

Were these Jefferson's last indicators of cognitive dissonance, or just plain hypocrisy? Indeed, historian John Boles questioned whether Jefferson "ever moderated the views on blacks expressed in *Notes on the State of Virginia.*"[98] His friends, Madison and Monroe, never changed their views about blacks either, but they both acted in conformity with them by not freeing slaves and by supporting the removal of those who were already free or about to be free from Virginia.

Most Free Blacks declined the opportunity to relocate to a continent they did not know. By 1816, when the American Colonization Movement was founded, people of African descent had been on the American continent nearly 200 years. This represented approximately ten generations since some of their ancestors had seen a mopane tree or consumed cassava.

TEN

*

Reversals, Registration, Kidnappings, and Social Interactions

B etween the years 1781, which brought the conclusion of the Revolutionary War, and 1861, which brought the beginning of the Civil War, the Free Black population continued to grow, acquire land and interact socially with their white neighbors and enslaved blacks. As it had been since 1619 with the first arrival of Africans, Virginia continued to be an integrated society. There were no restrictions on the land that Free Blacks could purchase and where they could live. Free Blacks were required, however, to register every three years and to keep their registration papers on them at all time to distinguish them from enslaved blacks, whose movement required the consent of their masters. While the Virginia legislature persistently banned consensual interracial sex and marriages during this period, it ignored master rape and violence as accoutrements of property ownership.

Post-Revolutionary War manumissions, coupled with births to Free Blacks and white women producing mulattos, contributed substantially to the growth of the Virginia Free Black population. Table 10-1 indicates that in 1790 nearly two percent of Virginia's population consisted of Free Blacks, thirty-nine percent of enslaved

blacks, and fifty-nine percent of whites. By 1820 the number of Free
Blacks had more than doubled.

Altogether, blacks encompassed over forty percent of all individuals living in Virginia in 1790, and the percentage had grown to
43% by 1820. Then the percentage declined as Virginia enacted policies encouraging Free Blacks to leave and owners to sell enslaved
blacks further South. As a matter of policy, the Virginia Legislature
sought to prevent the state from becoming a majority black state, as
was the case in South Carolina, or a supermajority enslaved state as
had been the case in Haiti when the slaves rebelled and killed most
of the whites.

TABLE 10-1. The Virginia Population from 1790–1860[1]

People	1790	1820	1840	1860
Free Blacks	12,866 (1.72%)	36,875 (3.46%)	49,841 (4%)	58,042 (3.6%)
Enslaved Blacks	292,627 (39.14%)	425,148 (40%)	448,988 (36%)	490,865 (30.8%)
Whites	442,117 (59.14%)	603,381 (56.63%)	740,968 (60%)	1,047,299 (65.6%)
Total	747,610	1,065,404	1,239,797	1,596,206

Despite the Free Black's relatively small percentage of overall blacks in the state, according to Professor Russell, "Of the free
[N]egro population of the United States, Virginia had about one
eighth."[2] Historian Luther Porter Jackson confirms Professor Russell's assessment in his book *Free Negro Labor and Property Holding
in Virginia, 1830–1860,* with the following statement, "The free Negro element in Virginia was always relatively large. In 1790 and 1800
Virginia led all the states in the number of free Negroes; in 1830 and
again in 1860 it held second place. At this last date the number of

free Negroes in Virginia was almost as great as the entire number of blacks in New York and New England combined."[3]

Fortunately Gideon Hill and his family had been freed by deed in 1787, right after manumissions were permitted and before the window started to close again. In the 1840 census when the American Colonization Society was actively recruiting Free Blacks to leave the country, Gideon Hill's household included eight "Free Colored Persons," with one male under 10, another between the ages of twenty and twenty-four, and Gideon who was between the ages of twenty-five and fifty-five.[4] His household also included three females under the age of ten, one female between the ages of ten and twenty-four, and one between the ages of twenty-five and fifty-five, presumably who was Gideon's wife.[5]

* * * * *

Reversals Inspired by Population Growth and Rebellions

The phase that began in the spirit of the Revolutionary War bringing freedom to whites from their British oppressors, and more manumissions of the enslaved, lasted a mere two decades. As the numbers of Free Blacks grew in certain communities, their presence caused social consternation in the Virginia legislature and brought another trend toward retrenchment that limited manumissions and restricted legal rights for Free Blacks. One concern was that the mere presence of Free Blacks encouraged enslaved blacks to seek freedom as well.[6] When the legislature began to restrict manumissions in 1691, it had threatened slaves with banishment after being set free,[7] and this happened again in the early 1800s.

In addition to population growth, a rebellion led by a slave named Gabriel in 1800 may have led to an era of retrenchment. Gabriel Prosser's plot to seize Richmond was thwarted and resulted in no white people being injured, but still Virginia hanged twenty-six blacks.[8] Gabriel may have been inspired by the 1791 Haitian rebellion led by Toussaint L'Ouverture, which resulted in the freedom of all the slaves three years later. While Napoleon sought to reestablish slavery in Haiti in 1802 by sending 60,000 troops to the island, L'Ouverture "led an effective guerilla resistance that, when combined with a deadly epidemic, kept the French army at bay."[9]

In 1806, Virginia legislators passed a law requiring slaves granted freedom to leave Virginia within a year and a day of receiving their emancipation.[10] This rule was further reinforced in the 1848 criminal code, when the Virginia legislature mandated:

> Any person emancipated from slavery since May 1, 1806, or claiming his right to freedom under an ancestor emancipated since that day, who shall remain in the state more than one year after his freedom accrued, and more than one year after he arrives at the age of twenty-one, or more than one year after the revocation of any lawful permission to remain shall forfeit his right to freedom and be sold as a slave.[11]

In *Family Bonds: Free Blacks and Re-enslavement Law in Antebellum Virginia*, historian Ted Maris-Wolf wrote about a substantial number of Free Blacks who chose to be re-enslaved in order to remain close by their relatives.[12]

The Acts of 1806 and 1848 discouraged whites from emancipating blacks, and blacks who purchased their enslaved relatives from manumitting them. Black women, like Sarah Spears, who acquired their enslaved husbands refrained from freeing them so they were not forced to leave Virginia. For similar reasons, black men, like Frank, who worked diligently to purchase their wives and children did not free them.

In some instances, the results could be particularly harsh. One commentator noted that the population of Free Black women may have exceeded the population of men of the same status, and thus, Free Black Women may have sought partnering with enslaved men.[13] Their children would be born free, but the enslaved man could be sold by his owner to another part of the country.

After Virginia passed its law encouraging blacks to leave, several northern and southern states passed laws refusing to accept recently freed blacks. Maryland, Kentucky, Delaware, Ohio, Indiana, Illinois, Missouri, North Carolina, and Tennessee all passed laws restricting emigration of blacks into their territories within twenty-five years of Virginia's harsh legislation.[14] South Carolina, where upwards of sixty percent of the population was enslaved during the antebellum period, also did not extend a cordial welcome to Virginia's expatriated Free Blacks.[15] To control those Free Blacks who remained, Virginia required them to register with the county clerk.

* * * * *

The Registration System

Because Free Blacks were required to register as of 1793,[16] physical descriptions are available of Gideon Hill and his kin. The Virginia General Assembly required all free Negroes and mulattoes in the Commonwealth to register with the clerk of the Court in the community in which they lived. The clerk recorded the name, age, color, status and emancipation details, such as by whom and in which county the registrant had been freed.[17] The law also required Free Negroes and mulattoes to re-register every three years. If they remained unregistered, they risked being jailed as runaway slaves. In 1834, the law was amended to require the clerk to note marks and scars in the description of the registrant.[18]

The advantage of the registries for future generations was that they provided descriptions of Free Blacks, something not available for whites or slaves. The registries were also potentially helpful to Free Blacks like Solomon Northup to confirm their identity. A Free Black stripped of his papers faced ominous results, but a registry meant a claim to freedom could eventually be verified.

The Free Negro Registry List of Dinwiddie County, 1850–1864, contained a description of Gideon at age sixty-nine as a person whose height was 5'6", his complexion was dark, and the scars on his body included one in the center of his forehead. The registry also stated that he obtained his freedom from Benjamin Crawley, by way of an emancipation deed. When Gideon Hill registered in 1856, he confirmed that he had obtained his freedom from Ben Crawley.[19]

In 1853, Nancy Hill registered as a daughter of Gideon Hill when she was sixteen. The registration record listed her color as black and her height as four-feet, eleven inches tall, she possessed no mark or scar on her head, face or hands, and she answered the question seeking how she acquired her freedom by replying that she was born free.[20]

Nancy's sister, Julia Hill, registered on March 9, 1855, and indicated that she was also born free. Julia was nineteen at the time, and her color was brown and her height noted at five-feet, six-inches. Unlike the flawless Nancy, Julia was described as having a small scar on her right wrist.[21] When Julia married John Bronwell on May 17, 1866, approximately a year after the conclusion of the Civil War, she listed her age as thirty-two and stated her parents were Celia and Gideon Hill.[22] The 1855 registry also included Nancy and Julia's oldest sister, Mary (the author's third great grandmother), who registered on July 26 when she was twenty-nine. Her height was listed as five foot and she had no apparent mark or scar. The Hill Family Tree can be found on page xiii.

* * * * *

Kidnappings

The registry system in Virginia and other states should have eliminated kidnappings because Free Blacks need only produce passes to prove the right to their freedom. Instead, the crime inflicted upon people of African descent for centuries continued unabated. Of the 25 million abducted from African villages against their will, only about 10 million landed in the Americas. Among those arriving in Virginia from 1619 to 1621 included Anthony Johnson, who was double kidnapped, first out of Angola and then on the high seas. Theft of people continued to be a primary fear for Free Blacks.

Aware of the post-Revolutionary War increase in manumissions, Virginia passed Chapter XXXVIII in 1788 to provide, "Whoever steals a free person, knowing him to be free, shall suffer death."[23] This statute, which prohibited Free Blacks and mulattoes from being stolen, was designed, according to the court in *Davenport v. Com.*,[24] to protect them in the enjoyment of their freedom.

According to the court, to preserve that freedom it was necessary to guard them against two classes of persons: first, those who might obtain a wrongful or illegal possession of them for the purpose of converting them to their own use; and second, those who having a rightful possession, or at least a possession, not illegal, might sell them as slaves.[25] Davenport was indicted and convicted of stealing a free mulatto boy that he knew at the time was free. The court found that the kidnapping completed the offense and was sufficient to convict, and that whether Davenport knew or didn't know of the boy's freedom need not be proven.[26]

Unfortunately, Free Blacks continued to be abducted by unscrupulous men seeking to profit from their quick sale into slavery. Gideon Hill's wife, Celia, had an unusual freedom struggle. Since her children had registered as free-born, that meant that Celia had to be a Free Black to pass on that status.

Among the Library of Virginia's original documents of over two-hundred-years old related to Free Blacks contain two items referencing a Celia. One item dated September 27, 1841, "and in the 66th year of our independence," was a request to the Courthouse to consider the application of Celia Holloway as a free woman of color who was emancipated since the first of May 1806 to remain in Petersburg, Virginia. By then, Free Blacks were required to leave Virginia within a year and a day of their emancipation unless they received special dispensation from the state legislature. Holloway had ignored the requirement for 34 years. This Celia Holloway was unlikely to be the person who married Gideon Hill because, by 1841, Gideon's Celia would have been calling herself Celia Hill or Mrs. Gideon Hill. Furthermore, the 1850 census records indicated that Gideon and his wife were living on a farm in Dinwiddie County, Virginia, and not in town.

The second item was dated June 8, 1809, and written as a letter from William Prentis "To whom it may concern." The handwritten document stated,

> *Sometime in the year 1795, as well as I recollect, the bearer Esther, with her daughter Celia, were brought to this town by water, and offered for sale as slaves by one Johnson. The Negroes, Esther and her daughter Celia, came to me and enquired if it was right to sell them as slaves, alledging that they were free, that they were brought away by force in the night, from the Eastern Shores of Maryland, put on board a vessel and arrived here with Johnson. Johnson came to me, and alledged that the said Negroes were slaves, that he offered them for sale as such, yet he could not show that they were slaves, nor any authority or instrument of writing by which he held them as such. He assured me, however, that he would go to the Eastern Shore of Maryland, and return here with satisfactory evidence of their being slaves—and left the Negroes with me. The Negroes have remained here ever since, subject to Johnson's claim—but as he never has come forward to claim them, I do perceive that they are entitled to their freedom. Some years ago, I was informed that Johnson was in Petersburg, but I never saw him.*
>
> *Petersburg, June 18, 1809*   *ss/William Prentis*

Because of the dates, this document most likely refers to the Celia who married Gideon Hill.

As a child in 1795, Celia was old enough to marry Gideon and bear his daughter Mary in 1826. The 1840 census listed Gideon's household as containing a female between the ages of 36 and 54, which indicated his wife was born between 1786 and 1804. The first year put her age closer to Gideon's. The next three census records provide a variety of ages for Celia and one misspelled her name as Sarah.[27] Perhaps one census taker phonetically spelled her name, and other census takers may have scrambled Celia's age because she was young-looking or she was not the one giving the information. The 1850 census listed her age as 40, meaning she would have been born about 1810, whereas the 1860 census listed her age as 64, indicating a birth in 1796. It would be unusual to age twenty-four years in a decade, but then the 1870 census listed her age as 68, meaning she aged four years in a decade.[28] The decennial censuses, thus, provided unreliable information as to Celia's age.

No matter the inaccuracies with decennial census information, Celia's story in Virginia clearly began when she and her mother were kidnapped in 1795 from the Eastern Shores of Maryland and brought to the Old Dominion by someone who proclaimed them slaves and abandoned them when his plan to sell them was challenged. Interestingly, they lived in William Prentis's residence for fourteen years awaiting Johnson's return before Prentis wrote this letter. Since Prentis was not their owner, he did not have the power to create a deed of manumission for Esther and Celia as Benjamin Crawley had done for Gideon and his relatives.

All Prentis could do is state the facts as he knew them. Once he heard that Johnson had returned to Petersburg but did not seek to collect Esther and Celia with sufficient proof, their claim to freedom must have made logical sense to Prentis. He released them with the only document he could, with a recitation of the facts as he knew them. Esther and Celia probably kept copies of Prentis' letter on or near themselves throughout their lives.

A subsequent search for information about William Prentis revealed that he had been a printer who edited the Virginia Gazette and Petersburg Intelligencer between 1786 and 1800. This was an occupation he shared with Founding Father Benjamin Franklin. Prentis had been born in England sometime between 1740 and 1765, according to PrenticeNet website. The 1810 census[29] listed him as living in a home with eight household members, which included him, his wife, three sons, one slave, and two other free persons (presumably Esther and Celia). The 1810 census also indicated he lived near at least eighty-two Free Blacks.

In 1800, a William Prentis had served as mayor of Petersburg during the time of Gabriel's rebellion. If the William Prentis who wrote the letter on behalf of Celia and Esther was the Petersburg mayor, that further validated its legal significance and explained why it was found among court archival documents in the Library of Virginia.

As the Prentis letter indicated, Esther was a Free Black, and thus she was either free born or manumitted by deed. Either way, Celia had been born free under the seventeenth century American rule that the child's legal status followed the mother. Celia passed that status on to her daughters who all registered as free born.

Esther and Celia's story of having been kidnapped from the Eastern Shores of Maryland bore a faint similarity to Solomon Northup's story in *Twelve Years a Slave*. Northup had been lured to Washington, D.C., from Sarasota, New York, with the promise of a musician's job. In the nation's capital, he was kidnapped and sold south to Louisiana.

Many Free Blacks lived in perpetual fear of slave catchers, not only those looking for runaways, but also those seeking to profit from legitimately freed blacks. A woman named Sarah Spears was faced with a difficult choice after having had children with an enslaved man named Bob.[30] Because of the rule of matrilineal descent, Sarah's children were born free because she was free. After purchasing Bob from his master, Sarah chose not to free him immediately, presumably to avoid the rule requiring newly freed slaves to depart Virginia within a year and a day of receiving manumission. As her death approached, Sarah willed Bob as a slave to their children so that Bob could remain in Virginia with his offspring. Thus, he did not risk being kidnapped and resold into slavery if he journeyed through surrounding hostile states. Nevertheless, the family contained a father as a slave with his children as his master!

✳ ✳ ✳ ✳ ✳

Land Ownership

Some Free Blacks became "prosperous owners of personal and real property."[31] There is even documentation supporting the proposition that many single free black women were landowners during the antebellum period.[32] Because Virginia declined to racially restrict land purchases, Gideon Hill's land acquisitions and sales during the first half of the 1800s could be tracked.

As a youth, Gideon Hill apprenticed as a blacksmith with Daniel Hardaway,[33] saved his money, and purchased land in Dinwiddie County, which was later annexed into Petersburg. In Dinwiddie County's General Index to Deeds, one document contained Gideon Hill's name as grantor and a Green J H W Reames Tr. as grantee for a Trust that was recorded on February 17, 1840.[34] Other Library of Virginia microfiche records showed deeds related to Gideon Hill's purchase of land using a deed of trust in 1843. The List of Land Tax within the county of Dinwiddie for 1849 contained a record of Hill's land holdings, stating that he owned fourteen acres near Cox Road in Dinwiddie and that the total value of the land and buildings was $28. The values ranged from $2 to $5,610 on this particular sheet. Hill paid taxes on his farm of fourteen acres near Cox Road.[35]

Hill's transformation from blacksmith to landowner was not uncommon. A Free Black named Arthur Lee, according to the records of Luther Porter Jackson,[36] had been born a slave in West Virginia and had worked out a deal with his master to hire himself out. He earned $1,200 for his master and eventually bought his freedom for $500 and that of his wife and child for an additional $350. By 1860, Arthur Lee owned 413 acres of land, a size that almost brought Lee's holdings to plantation status, which at that time required a minimum of 500 acres of land.

Other historians confirmed that Free Blacks possessed full rights to transfer property.[37] Ellen Katz observed that the Virginia state legislature, during the antebellum period, never racially restricted land ownership and the accompanying rights. She found that Cumberland County's free black residents "engaged in numerous land transactions during this period."[38] Indeed, she documented "seventy-six acquisitions of land by free black residents of Cumberland County between 1782 and 1863."[39]

In his research, Luther Porter Jackson refuted the belief by many whites that the bulk of land ownership was in the hands of mulattoes. He analyzed counties, and concluded that in Isle of Wight County, with the most complete records, 80% of the landowners were black rather than mulatto.[40] He found that the Negro race as a whole was of a darker hue before the American Revolution than after and this impacted land ownership. When Jackson surveyed the totality of black ownership in property in Virginia's cities and counties, he found the total result runs strongly in favor of the black element rather than the mulatto as owners of property.[41]

Many Free Blacks chose to live in cities, and tended to concentrate in the eastern half of the state.[42] In Petersburg, Free Blacks constituted about a fourth of all blacks, and about ten percent of the entire town in 1790. By 1830, the city contained 2,032 Free Blacks (24%), 2,850 enslaved blacks (34%), and 3,440 whites (41%).[43]

Gideon Hill lived on a farm in Dinwiddie County until his death. The Library of Virginia's microfiche records include the deed from 1856 when Gideon's heirs (listed as his wife Celia, and their children Mary, Julia, Edwin, Nancy, Gid, Sam, and Melville) sold the property following his passing.[44] After Celia and their children sold Gideon's farm, the adults purchased replacement property in Petersburg. Among the landowners in the town at that time were Celia Hill, Gideon's widow, and their grandson John Hill.[45] Celia had purchased her land in 1857 for $775 and by 1860 it had a value of $800, whereas John's land had been purchased in 1856 for $70 and had increased in value to $500.[46] Perhaps the values reflected the location of the land. Just prior to her father's death, Mary Hill purchased 30 acres in 1854. She paid $50 and by 1860 the value had risen to $400.[47]

The 1870 census records showed that Celia, Mary and Nancy lived near each other until Celia's death. A newspaper listed her as the widow of Reverend Gideon Hill, thus adding another profession to the free black man who began making money as a blacksmith and later became a farmer.

✳ ✳ ✳ ✳ ✳

Social Interactions

Throughout the antebellum period and until the Civil War, Free Blacks and whites socialized in Virginia as neighbors, conducted business, and sometimes, as discussed earlier, engaged in forbidden coupling. In the early 1600s, there had been Free Blacks who were accorded privileges equal to those of whites.[48] This indicates an early colonial period of easy interactions between the races.

Churches were integrated. First Baptist Church in Petersburg was founded in 1774. It is the oldest African-American congregation in the Nation. One part of its unusual history is that both Nat Turner and Dr. Martin Luther King, Junior, preached from its pulpit, albeit over a century apart. After Turner's insurrection on August 21, 1831, Virginia required a white person be present at all church meetings. First Baptist Church held services for whites, Free Blacks and enslaved blacks. White ministers led the church between 1842 and 1865.

Gideon and Celia Hill worshiped at Gillfield Church, which was founded in 1788. After Gabriel's rebellion in 1800, blacks and whites worshiped together because blacks were forbidden to congregate in groups of 20 or more without the presence of a white person. Gillfield Church's last white pastor was The Reverend William N. Robinson who served from 1858 to 1865. Gillfield Church remains in close proximity to First Baptist Church.

The Old Documents room of the Library of Virginia possesses material connected to Gillfield Church, including an old ledger of the church rolls. Mary Hill's name is listed under the column of individuals who had their church membership reinstated, meaning that her rights had once been stripped. Mary's rights as a member of Gillfield Baptist Church were likely revoked because she had had an interracial relationship that produced two mulatto children, both of whom were born free because she was free.

This can be inferred because Mary Hill was designated in the 1850 free inhabitants of Virginia census[49] as black and her sons John and George Hill as mulattos. This meant that their father was most likely white. Mary had two children by this man in an era when whites and blacks could not legally marry and thus legitimize their relationship and their children. In the 1860 census, John and George are listed as living as laborers in the home of a white male who might have been biologically connected to them.

✳ ✳ ✳ ✳ ✳

Interracial Couplings, Adultery, and Friendships

The births of John and George Hill exemplify that blacks and whites continued to have consensual sex after the Revolutionary War. Sometimes these couplings led white spouses to file petitions for divorce. During this time, divorce petitions were decided by the Virginia legislatures. In *Notorious in the Neighborhood: Sex and Families across the Color Line in Virginia, 1787–1861*, historian Joshua Rothman studied the cases of dozens of Virginia men and women who accused their spouses of interracial adultery.[50] In one instance, the man said his wife's liaison with a person of color occurred in his home and "on his bed."[51] A man named Howard "did not want to believe the reports circulating in the neighborhood but could no longer delude himself after he came home one night and discovered his wife naked and in bed with a free man of color."[52]

Likewise, many a wife who thought she had married a man from a "respectable family" was surprised when he engaged in interracial adultery. One wife accused her husband of running off with another man's slave, only to be caught and prosecuted for "attempted theft of property."[53] Washington Rowland slept in the same bed and in the same room with his enslaved mistress as his wife, while Lucy Norman reported that her husband James kissed his enslaved mistress, Maria, in front of her.[54] When Lucy complained about Maria's presence at their dinner table, James told Lucy that Maria "was as good and worthy as" she, and that if Lucy "did not like his course of conduct to leave his house and take herself to some place she liked better."[55]

In 1814, the Virginia legislature passed Chapter XCVIII to dissolve the marriage of Richard and Peggy Jones, "provided that a jury find that the child of Peggy is not the child of Richard, but is the offspring of a man of color."[56] This meant that the child had to be brought before a jury of white men, since women and Negroes were prohibited from serving on juries, to examine the child and vote on whether Richard or a man of color impregnated Peggy. In his divorce petition, Richard alleged that the baby "could not be the offspring of your petitioner or of any other white man."[57] This might have been a humiliating procedure for all concerned, including Richard, because men from his community were required to assess whether his wife had fornicated with a person of color and produced a child that did not belong to him. Yet Richard seemed to have come into a form of acceptance about the situation because his petition claimed the fact that his wife's daughter had a black father was "notorious in the neighborhood."[58]

Other married white women who delivered mulatto children faced dissolution of their marriages.[59] In 1803, the Virginia legislature passed Chapter 6, which provided, "The marriage between Benjamin Butt, Jr., and a certain Lydia Bright, who is of [a] respectable family, and was at the time of the marriage supposed to be unsullied in her reputation, is dissolved because Lydia has been delivered of a mulatto child and has publicly acknowledged that the father of the child is a slave."[60]

Subsequent to her divorce, Lydia Bright was probably spurned by her family and friends since she was no longer "unsullied in her reputation." She may also have been forced to give the child to either the church or his enslaved father to rear. If given to the church, the child became an indentured servant for a number of years before receiving ultimate freedom because his mother was free. If handed over to his enslaved father, however, the child might have been raised as a slave in service to his father's master. Lydia could also have chosen to raise her child while suffering rebukes from her neighbors. If she traveled with slaves outside of her community, then other whites might have assumed the child belonged to a slave.

In some instances, the man waited until his wife had produced more than one biracial child before petitioning for divorce. According to Rothman, "The wives of Thomas Cain and Lewis Bourn had not one but two children with black men."[61] Sarah Hall produced three biracial children before her patient husband, Richard, petitioned for divorce in 1838.[62] Sarah's relationship with a black man began before she married Richard in 1829 and her first biracial child was born six months after their wedding.[63]

Perhaps Lydia Bright, Peggy Jones, and these other wives were fortunate that their husbands chose to seek legal dissolution of their marriages after they had given birth to children of color. In modern times, it may be hard to contemplate the shock the husbands experienced after seeing what they thought were their children for the first time. Not only had their wives deceived them, but they had also, presumably, betrayed their race by having sexual relations with persons of color.

Nevertheless, the Virginia legislature did not always grant such divorce petitions. Rothman calculated that the legislature dissolved marriages for only 70% of white men and 55% of white women charging their spouses with interracial adultery.[64] Thus, 30% of white males and 45% of white females were forced to remain married to their spouses in these situations. Although the legislature frequently passed statutes outlawing interracial sex, it often chose not to enforce its own rules.

Virginia governors also intervened in marital disputes. In 1841, Alexander Wells, a white man, sold his white wife for a dollar so that he could marry another woman, which he did.[65] He was charged with bigamy, convicted and sentenced to two years in the penitentiary. As Suzanne Lebsock wrote in *The Free Women of Petersburg*, "Immediately after sentence was pronounced, however, counsel for the defense, the prosecuting attorney, the jury, and several local officials united in petitioning the governor for clemency. Alexander was pardoned on June 25, 1842."[66]

*   *   *   *   *

Social interactions between free blacks and whites were further evidenced by the number of Virginia citizens who petitioned the legislature to permit newly freed slaves to remain in the state. In his book, Professor Russell mentioned the plea of the inhabitants of Lynchburg for Pleasant Rowan, a free colored carpenter and mechanic, for "'his loss would be felt by the community'" and the 120 whites who petitioned to keep Daniel Warner, "a free [N]egro barber of Warrenton."[67] Another appeal filed on behalf of Harriet Cook was signed by nearly 100 whites that included seven justices of the peace, five ex-justices, sixteen merchants, six lawyers and a postmaster.[68] Their entreaty said, "'It would be a serious inconvenience to a number of the citizens of Leesburg to be deprived of her services as a washerwoman and in other capacities in which, in consequence of her gentility, trust-worthiness, and skill she is exceedingly useful.'"[69]

White folks from the town of Halifax pleaded that Fortune Thomas, a free colored woman, had rendered her services for baking cakes and tarts and making candies indispensable.[70] The petitioners added, "she has been earnestly assured by the ladies that they can in no measure dispense with her assistance and that no party or wedding can well be given without great inconvenience should her shop be broken up and discontinued."[71]

All of these effective petitions to the legislature confirm the presence of successful businesses run by Free Blacks in the state of Virginia. These were enterprises that were so appreciated by whites that they were willing to battle in the legislature to keep the owners within Virginia. Because they were free, Pleasant, Daniel, Harriet, and Fortune could employ their skills and talents for the benefit of themselves and their communities.

In 1830, Free Blacks owned 678 farms and by 1860 that number had increased to 1,202 in Virginia.[72] In addition to working as blacksmiths and farmers (like Gideon Hill), Free Blacks labored as shoemakers, mechanics, carpenters, and sailors.

In some situations, newly freed blacks like Celia Holloway—who didn't register for 34 years—just chose to remain in the state and they were not apprehended.[73] No petitions were filed on their behalf. This was merely one instance of several indicating disconnects between the legal rules and their enforcement. In her article *African-American Freedom in Antebellum Cumberland County, Virginia*, Ellen Katz argued, "white perceptions of free blacks embodied in the state's laws are not readily evident in the daily interactions between whites and free blacks in [Cumberland] county."[74]

These friendly connections occurred at a time when Virginia slowly stripped away more rights from Free Blacks from 1802 to 1865, including their privileges to own weapons, freely assemble, and travel within and outside of the state. Ira Berlin writes in his forward to Paul Heinegg's book, "[F]ree blacks found their legal rights circumscribed. In various colonies, they were barred from voting, sitting on juries, serving in the militia, carrying guns, owning dogs, or testifying against whites."[75]

One might assume that if blacks could not testify against white oppressors, it was almost impossible to convict a white person for harming a black person. However, there were instances of whites who witnessed crimes against blacks and reported them to authorities. In *Cato v. Scruggs*, after Lawrence Cato, a Free Black, sued Valentine Scruggs, a white woman, for illegally entering and detaining his five-acre estate, his white neighbors testified on his behalf. An all-white jury decided he could regain possession of his property and be reimbursed by Scruggs for his cost in suing her.[76] In 1834, another Free Black property owner, Judith Lipscomb, received a jury verdict in her favor.[77]

But there were many other incidents where Free Blacks were less successful in their attempts to bring whites to justice for violating their legal rights. For example, Ellen Katz cites the 1847 lawsuit that Kitty Lipscomb, a Free Black female property holder, filed against William Bradley, a white man, after he allegedly assaulted her.[78] The complaint alleged that Bradley beat Lipscomb with "clubs, sticks, and fists."[79] Lipscomb sought $200 in damages, and three whites were summoned to testify. The jury found in favor of Lipscomb but only awarded her damages of $6.66 plus costs.[80]

Successful petitions positively impacted lives. As mentioned earlier, a Free Black by the name of Frank died before emancipating his enslaved widow, Patience, and their three children.[81] It took a petition to the legislature in 1810 to save them from being re-enslaved. The legislature acknowledged that Frank had purchased his family with "meritorious industry,"[82] and declared, "it is enacted by the General Assembly that Patience and the children shall be free."[83] Frank probably did not free Patience and their children because they would have been forced to leave the state.

Newly freed black men who petitioned the legislature to remain in Virginia often pointed out that their wives and children were slaves.[84] There were some legal rules prohibiting marriage between free black women and enslaved men,[85] although women like Sarah Spears continued to form such relationships. Many petitions were brought seeking to permit Free Blacks to remain in the state. Some were successful while others failed. For example, in 1810, the legislature permitted Pompey Branch, to remain as a free person of color in the state.[86] In 1811, the legislature permitted Jingo and James Lott, free men of color, to remain in the state and also Hannah, who was liberated by William Turner, to remain in the state.[87] But the following year, while it honored the provision of a will freeing the slave Jacob, the Virginia legislature refused to permit him to remain in the state.[88] Without legislative history, it is difficult to determine why the legislature granted certain petitions but denied others.

✳   ✳   ✳   ✳   ✳

Restrictions on Freedom Movement

While Free Blacks had more freedom of movement than enslaved blacks, Virginia continued to pass restrictions during the decades following the Revolutionary War. Chapter 99 passed in 1838 provided, "If free Negroes, whether infant or adult, go beyond the limits of the Commonwealth to be educated, it shall not be lawful for them to return; if infants they shall be bound out as apprentices until twenty-one years, and then sent out of the state; if adults they shall be sent out of the Commonwealth."[89] Ten years later, Chapter 120 (1848) provided, "Any free person of color who shall migrate from the state, or who shall for the purpose of being educated be sent from the state, or who shall for any purpose go to a non-slaveholding state, shall be no longer entitled to residence in Virginia."[90] Thus, Free Blacks were threatened with banishment if they or their children left the state to be educated.

In the article, *"Rather than the Free": Free Blacks in Colonial and Antebellum Virginia,* Judge Leon Higginbotham analyzed the denial of the rights to hold public office, to vote, to possess weapons, to travel, and to associate with other blacks, both the free and the enslaved.[91] When the Virginia legislature mandated that if Free Blacks left Virginia to obtain an education in the North they could not return to the state, Higginbotham and Bosworth considered these rules were "enacted out of fear that an enlightened free black population threatened both white Virginians' property interests and the stability of slavery."[92]

Such rules discouraged Free Blacks from sending their children to northern states to be educated because they could not return. Since Virginia had passed prior restrictions on Free Blacks' ability to obtain an education within the state, this ensured that most Free Blacks remained illiterate unless they were taught by literate relatives or by religious organizations such as the Quakers.

South Carolina restricted the freedom of movement even more than Virginia. In her book *Amelioration and Empire*, Christa Dierksheide wrote about South Carolina, the state with the largest overall percentage of blacks: "[I]n 1822, the legislature passed laws that . . . levied an annual tax of $50 on each free black man, prevented free blacks from re-entering the state after they had left, and stipulated that all free blacks must have white guardians or face expulsion from the state."[93] Dierksheide considered the Negro Seaman's Act to be even more draconian because it "allowed local authorities to imprison free black sailors while their ships remained docked at a South Carolina port."[94] Perhaps this was done to prevent them from spreading news from the North.

✳ ✳ ✳ ✳ ✳

Although historian Ira Berlin referred to Free Blacks as "slaves without masters" in the title to his book,[95] from a black person's perspective there was a huge difference between being free and being enslaved, despite the restrictions on Free Blacks. It is this difference that made Solomon Northup's book, *Twelve Years a Slave*, and the major motion picture, *12 Years a Slave*, so compelling a literary and entertainment experience. Northup was someone who had been born free, only to be kidnapped by those seeking profit from selling him into slavery.[96] The difference between Northup's life as a Free Black and his life as an enslaved Black was dramatic.

In his book *Freedom Has a Face*, Professor Kirt von Daacke questioned Berlin's view of Free Blacks "as only nominally free and trapped in a precarious existence" and repeated in Ulrich Bonnell Phillips' work *American Negro Slavery*.[97] Von Daacke preferred, instead, to follow the growing body of scholarship that highlighted the economic freedoms and opportunities available to Free Blacks.[98] He noted that some scholars have found a "startling degree of economic and financial success among individual African Americans."[99] To lend further credence to this view of Free Blacks, von Daacke examined the economic and social successes, as well as failures, of Free Blacks in one rural antebellum county in Virginia.[100]

Berlin, nonetheless, also opined, "No matter how hard whites squeezed black liberty, the irreducible differences between freedom and slavery remained. Freedom allowed blacks to reap the rewards of their own labor, to develop a far richer social life, and to enjoy the many intangible benefits of liberty."[101] Further, he wrote, "With hard work, skill, and luck, some free Negroes climbed off the floor of Southern society, acquired wealth and social standing."[102]

Thus the eight decades between the end of the Revolutionary War in 1781 and the beginning of the Civil War in 1861 brought a mixture of results for Free Blacks. It would take a Northern general who had married into a southern slaveholding family to successfully bring freedom to those who remained in bondage.

ELEVEN

The Civil War and Jim Crow

On the eve of the Civil War in 1860, the Free Black population had doubled to nearly four percent despite Virginia's policy of deliberately reducing the number of blacks in its territory. The 1860 decennial census confirmed that 58,042 Free Blacks, together with the enslaved population of 490,865, in Virginia were confined largely to the eastern half of the state.[1] There, 600,000 whites lived, numbering just slightly above the total black population of 548,907. Thus, the Free Black population came into contact with only about one-half of the white population.

All total, there were sixteen Virginia counties where a large proportion of the black inhabitants were free.[2] Among the counties with significant proportions of Free Blacks were Accomac County, where 3,392 (or 42.4%) of the 8,000 black inhabitants were free, and James County where 926 (or 33.5%) of 2,764 blacks were free. Perhaps most astounding, in Nanesmond County 2,470 (81%) of the 3,051 blacks were free.[3]

Because the enslaved population had declined, the percentage of total blacks in Virginia had dropped to thirty-four percent while the white population had risen to nearly sixty-six percent. This shift occurred because, according to historian John Chester Miller, "from 1830 to 1860, Virginia sold over three hundred thousand slaves to buyers outside the state—a diaspora comparable in scope to some of the great mass migrations of history."[4] This shift ensured that Virginia did not join "South Carolina in shifting from a predominantly white to a predominantly black population."[5]

✳   ✳   ✳   ✳   ✳

Consequences of the Louisiana Purchase

The enslaved Africans who were sold south became victims of Jefferson's Louisiana Purchase. While the acquisition doubled the size of the United States at a cost of less than one cent per acre, the Louisiana Purchase set the stage for the Indian Wars, which removed Indians from their ancestral lands. Once the territory was mostly cleared of the indigenous owners, who were victimized by the land grab accompanying the Louisiana Purchase, whites moved in. They set up plantations and imported millions of Africans, primarily from other states, like Virginia, to farm the land and pick the cotton.

Although Congress's ban on the intercontinental slave trade took effect in 1808 during the last year of Thomas Jefferson's presidency, slavers continued to bring in Africans from the continent and the sugar islands as the demand for slaves increased. Cudjo Lewis was among the last black cargo brought to this country on the *Clotilda* around 1860. Lewis' story was captured by Zora Neale Hurston in *Barracoon* in 1927, and published in 2018.[6] Thus, while the Free Black population was growing primarily through natural increase and manumissions after the conclusion of the Revolutionary War, the enslaved population grew exponentially despite the moratorium on the international slave trade. In classic economic formation, as the demand for slaves to till the cotton fields rose, their prices increased.

In Table 11-1, historian Edward E. Baptiste researched and estimated (as indicated with asterisks) the relationship between the growing enslaved population and the increasing percentage of enslaved people as a share of the wealth over the seven decades between 1790 and 1860. Note that during the decades leading up to the Civil War, nearly 20% of United States wealth was connected to the forced labor of people of African origin.

TABLE 11-1. Enslaved People as a Percentage of U.S. Wealth[7]

Year	Total U.S. Wealth (Millions of Dollars)	Enslaved Population	Wealth in Slaves (Millions of Dollars)	Enslaved People as Share of All U.S. Wealth
1790	1,150	800,000*	200*	0.174
1800	2,400	1,000,000*	250*	0.104
1810	Unknown	1,191,000	316	—
1820	Unknown	1,538,022	610	—
1830	3,825	2,009,043	577	0.151
1840	5,226	2,487,355	997	0.191
1850	7,135	3,204,313	1,286	0.180
1860	16,160	3,953,760	3,059	0.189

Observe also the expansion of slavery between 1790 and 1860. While Baptiste estimated (as indicated by asterisks) the enslaved population and the wealth in slaves in millions of dollars in 1790 and 1810, his 1810 numbers represented results from the decennial population census. The 1810 census, indicating 1,191,000 enslaved Africans, was the first taken following the ban on the intercontinental slave trade in 1808. Yet by 1860 on the eve of the Civil War, the number of enslaved had almost quadrupled to 3,953,760. Baptiste's book, *The Half That Has Never Been Told: Slavery and the Making of American Capitalism*, recounts a horrific tale explaining how Virginia and other states separated mothers from their children and husbands from their families to force the migration of its enslaved population further south and west.

Some of the first Africans who arrived in Virginia in 1619 and in the years thereafter could perhaps be considered lucky because they were kidnapped on the high seas and spared the fate of being taken to Portuguese Brazil, Spanish Veracruz, and the sugar islands, where life was short and hard. There were no such unexpected detours, such as those experienced by the first Africans in 1619, for those being sold after 1810. The enslaved were walked or shipped in chains to misery, torture, rape, and death, as whites' invested in slaves to augment their wealth and that of the country. According to Baptiste, "African-American and white abolitionists identified family separations and the exposure of women to sexual abuse as two of the most devastating impacts of the domestic slave trade."[8]

What happened in the western cotton fields fulfilled Jefferson's belief that among slavery's evils was the potential to "debauch the morals of the master" because "whites were utterly demoralized by the intoxicating sense of power it engendered."[9] If "power corrupts, and absolute power corrupts absolutely," then this expansion of slavery was set up to create a total abuse of power because there were few checks on masters' behavior toward their slaves. In the new territory, masters could do with their slaves what they wanted. Some raped the women, and sold the resulting children. Only when catastrophe struck for a master, and a slave met violence with violence, did society take note.

An example can be found in the case of Celia[10] (not the wife of Gideon Hill) who grew tired of her master's rapes in Missouri. Robert Newsom purchased her as a fourteen-year old on the auction block and forced himself on her during the wagon ride back to his home. After enduring five-years of sexual violence, Celia struck Newsom with a large stick over and over until he moved no more. Then Celia chopped up Newsom, burned his body in her fireplace, and offered chestnuts to Newsom's grandson to help her remove the large amount of ashes from her fireplace. Celia was tried and convicted because, as an enslaved woman, she had no honor to protect and thus could not resist her master's advances. In other words, Newsom had absolute power over his property and legally

Celia had no right to counterattack his assertions of dominion over her body.

Found guilty of murder, Celia was sentenced to hang. Some white citizens who sympathized with her plight broke her out of jail to prevent implementation of the death sentence, but she was recaptured and hanged.[11]

Such horrid cases often meant that the only check on the master's power was asserted by slaves themselves. Indeed, some whites lived in fear of being poisoned, the method one slave used to kill President James Madison's grandfather who apparently exercised brutality toward the slave. Others were concerned about potential rebellions, such as those of Gideon Prosser, Nat Turner, and John Brown that sought to end their rule.

Instead of a gradual elimination of slavery as Washington, Jefferson and other national leaders had envisioned, the institution expanded to the detriment of those of African descent and set the stage for war. Since the country began with the arrival of the English in 1607 and the Africans in 1619, and the Virginia legislature transformed the status of subsequently arriving Africans from indentured servants to servants for life in 1670, perhaps it was not surprising that Virginia would play an outsized role in the Civil War.

After the South's secession, Virginia commissioned General Robert E. Lee, whose military skills were so valued that President Abraham Lincoln had sought him for the Union, to lead the army of Northern Virginia. The Confederate capital was situated in Richmond. Two Virginia cities, Petersburg and Richmond, would be the sites of the war's last two major battles. And Lee surrendered to General Grant in a brick house on the outskirts of Appomattox Court House[12] in Virginia.

By the eve of the Civil War, there was no middle ground left that could lead to the gradual emancipation of four million blacks held in bondage. The Founding Fathers had kicked the can containing the elimination of slavery down the road and it ended at the Appomattox Court House, where two slaveholding generals met.

Lee had married into the Custis family and became the caretaker of the slaves and issue of slaves that Martha Dandridge Custis
Washington, wife of the first president, was obliged to divide among
her children. Like earlier antislavery-slaveholders, Lee described
slavery as "a moral & political evil" while also saying that he thought
"it however a greater evil to the white man than to the black race."[13]
Benjamin Franklin had previously expressed his opinion that slavery led white children to become disgusted with labor. In his autobiography, *Up From Slavery*, Booker T. Washington shared a similar
view. He wrote that because the "whole machinery of slavery was
so constructed as to cause labor . . . to be looked upon as a badge
of degradation, of inferiority." He added that the slave system took
"the spirit of self-reliance and self-help out of white people."[14] The
white boys were not taught "a single trade or special line of productive activity," and the white "girls were not taught to cook, sew, or
to take care of a house."[15] Further, he said, the whites lack of skills
caused "pity among the slaves for [their] former owners."[16]

Notwithstanding Robert E. Lee's views on the harm that slavery
caused whites, he inflicted pain on the men and women he held in
bondage. Unlike George and Martha Dandridge Custis Washington who believed in keeping enslaved families together, Lee broke
up every family but one on the estate by hiring off slaves to other
plantations.[17] On his plantation, Lee had his overseer whip blacks
severely and then wash their lacerated naked flesh with brine, or
salted water, to compound the torture.[18]

During his Gettysburg campaign, Lee enabled the kidnapping of
Pennsylvania's Free Blacks to be sold into slavery in the South. At
the crater outside of Petersburg during the long siege of the city, Lee
did not stop his men from slaughtering black soldiers who sought
to surrender. Lee talked a lot about God while his behavior toward
other humans evoked the suffering of Jesus of Nazareth.

For all his fame as a strategic thinker, Lee would be out-strategized
by Grant. Three years after their encounter in Appomattox Courthouse, Ulysses S. Grant was elected the 18th president of the United
States in 1868.

* * * * *

Free Black Soldiers in the Civil War

Black Union soldiers captured by General Robert E. Lee and marched through the streets of Petersburg "to the slurs and jeers of the southern crowd"[19] were among the nearly 200,000 Free Blacks from all across the country who mustered into the Union army to liberate 4,000,000 people from bondage. Enslaved blacks ran away and joined the Union cause as well.

Unlike in the Revolutionary War where blacks entered the conflict from the beginning, it was only as recruitment for white soldiers waned in the North amid a public perception that the war would not end that President Abraham Lincoln permitted northern Free Blacks to enlist. Dissimilar to the Revolutionary War, where Free Blacks fought alongside whites in the North, the Union army volunteers were segregated. They were designated the United States Colored Troops beginning with the 54th Massachusetts division regiment assault on Ft. Wagoner in July 1863. The 54th division was memorialized in the film *Glory*[20] staring actor Denzel Washington, who won his first Oscar playing a Free Black Union soldier. Led by white officers, the Colored Troops fought bravely, and in so doing "shattered every myth the South's slave empire was built on: the happy docility of slaves, their intellectual inferiority, their cowardice, their inability to compete against whites."[21]

Another Revolutionary War situation repeated itself when toward the end of the conflict the Confederate States of America offered enslaved blacks their freedom if they joined their cause. Such an offer, which came a few months before the Confederacy collapsed, seemed to undercut the claim of many Confederate leaders of their rights to enslave blacks. By accepting them into their armed forces, the Confederates gave blacks weapons, which they had forbidden others to do during peacetime.

Descendants of color of Founding Fathers Thomas Jefferson and Aaron Burr contributed to the cause of liberation. John Wayles

(Hemings) Jefferson, the son of Eston Hemings Jefferson and grandson of Sally Hemings and Thomas Jefferson, became a lieutenant colonel in the Union army. According to historians Gordon-Reed and Onuf, he "pleaded with members of his Wisconsin cohort not to tell his story, lest it become known that he was part African-American, and thus would be unable to rise through the ranks as he did."[22] Raymond Burr, the grandson of John Pierre Burr and great-grandson of Aaron Burr, became a colonel in the post-Civil War black militia.[23]

One Free Black was so determined to join the Union cause that he added a few years to actual age of sixteen to be eligible. From his home in Petersburg, George W. Hill, the grandson of Gideon Hill, travelled to Norfolk to enlist.

✳ ✳ ✳ ✳ ✳

Free Blacks Who Lived Through the Civil War

Before George Hill left his mother Mary and his grandmother Celia in Petersburg in 1863 to muster into the United States Colored Troops, these Hill family members were among the 3,164 Free Blacks living in Petersburg in the 1860 census. The city also possessed 5,680 slaves and a number of whites about equal to the total black population.[24] Petersburg was the sight of the last large-scale battle in the Civil War. Since Petersburg supplied Richmond, and was the hub of five railroads, Grant reasoned that "If Petersburg fell, Richmond and Lee's army fell, and the war would hasten to a speedy conclusion."[25]

The campaign in Petersburg was not swift. In Grant's memoirs, he wrote in 1864, "The advance of the Army of the Potomac reached the James on the 14th of June."[26] By 1865, Grant added, "During the night of April 2d our line was intrenched from the river above to the river below. I ordered a bombardment to be commenced the next morning at five A.M., to be followed by an assault at six o'clock; but the enemy evacuated Petersburg early in the morning."[27] Grant and General Meade entered Petersburg on April 3rd. The speedy con-

clusion to the war that Grant had predicted came when Richmond
fell soon thereafter.

According to Mrs. Elizabeth Keckley, "it was reported that the
rebel capital had surrendered to colored troops."[28] Mrs. Keckley was
born a slave in Dinwiddie, Virginia,[29] endured the sorrows of being
flogged and raped before becoming a mother of a mulatto child.[30]
She was able to purchase her freedom and that of her son by hiring
out her skills as a dressmaker. Eventually moving to Washington
City, as the District of Columbia was then known, Keckley became
a prominent dressmaker to Mrs. Robert E. Lee, Mrs. Jefferson Davis,
and Mrs. Abraham Lincoln. It was her association with the First
Lady that led her to be invited to City Point and to tour Petersburg
with the sixteenth president. Keckley wrote, "Getting out of the car,
the President and those with him went to visit the forts and other
scenes, while I wondered off by myself in search of those whom I
had known in other days. War, grim-visaged war, I soon discovered
had brought many changes to the city. . . . The scenes suggested
painful memories."[31]

In a strange irony, Confederate President Jefferson Davis was
captured wearing one of Mrs. Keckley's chintz wrappers as a dis-
guise.[32] Keckley had made the dress for Davis's wife when they lived
in Washington City and he served in the Senate. This was a short
time before the commencement of the Civil War.

By their existence, Free Blacks, like Mrs. Keckley, disproved racist
remarks that national leaders and other whites made about people of African descent. Free Blacks like Gideon Hill and his family
managed their lives and their property. They thus did not need to
be treated as children. Even denied the right to vote and participate
in civic affairs after 1723, Free Blacks continued their lives under
a rubric of strict rules. As difficult as their lives were, the enslaved
blacks, like those who toiled and were whipped by and on behalf of
General Robert E. Lee, were treated much worse.

About Free Blacks, Frederick Douglas wrote, "The most telling,
the most killing refutation of slavery, is the presentation of an in-
dustrious, enterprising, upright, thrifty, and intelligent free black

population."[33] An example of this industriousness can be found by the activities of James Hill, a relative of Gideon Hill, who was also freed by Benjamin Crawley on January 25, 1787, in the same deed of emancipation.[34] After receiving his freedom, James Hill purchased his wife Sarah and her two children Sally and Moses from a William Mosely of Chesterfield County, Virginia, on March 1, 1798. James and Sarah had two additional children together before she died. In 1812, James Hill freed all four children by deed in Tennessee where he had subsequently moved.[35] To save money to purchase his wife and her two children took financial diligence, and then to set all four of her biological children free was a testament to James Hill's generosity of spirit.

The stories inherent in the lives of Free Blacks reminds us that the war that caused the loss of over 600,000 American lives and maimed millions others could have been avoided. Virginia did not have to pass the 1670 law designating subsequently arriving Africans as servants for life, or slaves, Virginia did not have to strip Free Blacks of the cornerstones of citizenship, including the right to vote, to educate their children, to freely associate, and to travel. Perhaps Free Blacks participating in the political process might have created a more just world for everyone. Some evidence for this assertion can be inferred from when, during the Reconstruction Era,[36] Free Black legislators led the charge to create public education for everyone. "The War of Northern Aggression," as the Southerners referred to the Civil War, could have perhaps been avoided had newly arriving Africans been accorded the same rights as the English indentured servants.

* * * * *

Jim Crow

Southern slaveholders did not slide silently into the good night and accept the massive loss of their wealth tied up in human capital. The newly freed and already freed blacks were not accorded full citizenship rights as Congress envisioned by passing the Thirteenth, Fourteenth, and Fifteenth Amendments to the Constitution. After a period of Reconstruction (1865–1877), southern legislatures, including the one in Virginia, replicated the legal and social challenges that Free Blacks had encountered for all blacks. The Jim Crow era followed the period of Reconstruction.

Indeed, the 1880s brought a period of segregation that had not existed before. From their arrival in 1619 and onward, Africans lived in the same structures, worked in the same fields, and fought in the same battles alongside their English counterparts. The Africans and English mated, had children together, and sometimes stood up for each other in tribunals and other legal proceedings.

With the hardships that followed the collapse of Reconstruction and its goal to equalize the social environment for the newly freed, more individuals sought to be released from the continuing negative repercussions associated with African heritage. Immediately after the Civil War, the Virginia legislature reiterated that people "having one-fourth or more Negro blood shall be deemed a colored person," and a person "having one-fourth or more Indian blood shall be deemed an Indian."[37]

In 1885, a Virginia County Court sentenced Isaac Jones, as a Negro, to the penitentiary for two years and nine months for the felonious marriage to Martha Gray, a white woman.[38] The marriage was considered "against the peace and dignity of the commonwealth" and violated a statute that provided, "Any white person who shall intermarry with a negro, and any negro who shall intermarry with a white person, shall be confined to the penitentiary not less than two nor more than five years."[39] Jones appealed his sentence on the grounds that the Court failed to prove that he was a Negro. Since the county produced no evidence that he was a Negro, the court said that he was presumed not to be, and therefore he was assumed innocent.[40] The court's rationale was that a man of mixed blood was not a Negro unless the Commonwealth proved that he had at least one-fourth of Negro blood in his veins. In this case, the Commonwealth had offered no evidence to prove its case.

By 1910, Virginia lowered the blood quantum separating blacks and whites to one-sixteenth of African blood.[41] Subsequently, the

Virginia legislature passed Chapter 371, to provide, "For the preservation of racial integrity" requiring registration certificates for
those born before June 14, 1912, to show their racial purity.[42] In
1930, the Virginia legislature lowered the percentage of blood quantum from one-sixteenth to one drop by providing, "Every person
in whom there is ascertainable any Negro blood shall be deemed a
colored person."[43] These changes are depicted in Table 11-2:

TABLE 11-2. The Virginia Legal Definitions of Negroes

Year	Percent of Negro Blood	Ancestor Requirement
1785	One Fourth	At least one grandparent
1910	One Sixteenth	At least one great-great grandparent
1930	One Drop	Any ancestor

The 1930 rule lowering the blood quantum defining who was a
Negro to one drop, or any ancestor, represented an epic low quan-
tity in Virginia. The irony of the 1930 rule is that currently, in the
age of DNA testing, a majority of the populations in many Southern
States might qualify as Negro. By contrast, at the end of the Civil
War in 1865, for example, only two states—South Carolina and
Mississippi—had majority black populations.

Companies like *Ancestry.com* and *23 and Me* can now isolate African DNA that connects individuals to their seventh and eighth
great-grandparents. An individual receives fifty percent of his or her
DNA from each parent, but still may have approximately 0.198125%
of their DNA from the 512 individuals who contributed to their
DNA at the level of seventh great-grandparents. Many whites who
thought they had Native American ancestry have been surprised to
discover their DNA contained no Native American blood, but instead one or more percentages of African blood. Conversely, blacks
who thought they were part Native American have been surprised
to discover their DNA contained no Native American blood, but
instead one or more percentages of European blood. These trace el-

ements are holdovers from long ago mixing of the races, sometimes as far back as the original arrivals from Africa in 1619.

While a person might look entirely white, one or more of their 512 seventh great-grandparents could have been African. Similarly, an individual might look completely black, yet one or more of their 512 seventh great-grandparents could have been English, European or Native American. Table 11-3 depicts the approximate DNA percentages that a person obtains from each ancestor.

TABLE 11-3. DNA Relatives and Percentages

Relatives	DNA Percentage from each relative	Relatives	DNA Percentage from each relative
2 parents	50%	64 fourth great-grandparents	1.5625%
4 grandparents	25%	128 fifth great-grandparents	0.78125%
8 great-grandparents	12.50%	256 sixth great-grandparents	0.390625%
16 great-great-grandparents	6.25%	512 seventh great-grandparents	0.198125%
32 third great-grandparents	3.125%	1024 eighth great-grandparents)	0.099%

Thus defining who belongs to which race is not as simple as looking at a person or examining who their great-great grandparents might have been. The 1930 Virginia one-drop rule would fail the tests of modern science.

Based on these misguided conceptions of race following the Civil War, governments and individuals continued to enact racial restrictions. The Jim Crow-era brought covenants written into land deeds prohibiting individuals from living in certain neighborhoods. Prior to the Civil War, Free Blacks and whites freely purchased land from each other and lived in the same neighborhoods.

In the South abounded separate schools, water fountains and bathrooms to remind people of African descent that they were "others." These laws prohibiting whites and blacks from drinking at the same water fountains were enacted as black women continued to nurse white children from their breast, just as Thomas Jefferson's children had been fed by Ursula Grainger.

The integrated immersion of peoples that began in 1619 with the arrival of 20 or odd Negroes on the shores of Virginia is a tale of legal twists and turns, progress toward equality and reversals that removed rights. Perhaps the best representation of this struggle can be found in the tale of John Punch, the African who ran away from his indentured servitude with two Europeans in 1640. When captured, the Europeans were punished with a few years added to their contract whereas Punch's contract was reformed to become one requiring service for life, or to become a slave. Punch's son changed his surname to Bunch, perhaps to escape the stigma of what happened to his father. The Bunch descendants married and mated with so many white people that they passed into white society long before Virginia enacted its one-drop rule in 1930.

A woman named Stanley Ann Dunham,[44] who came into this world as the tenth great-granddaughter of John Punch and thus a descendant of Free Blacks and enslaved blacks, married a Kenyan. Their son, Barack Hussein Obama, became the 44th president of the United States.

Story Replication[1]

The story of the Free Blacks and how all freed slaves were treated would find historical replication in how Jews were treated in Nazi Germany and how blacks were regulated in Apartheid South Africa. Rules such as defining who was a Negro in Colonial Virginia, which became stricter under Jim Crow, were eventually used by the Nazis to delineate who was considered a Jew and by the White South African government to distinguish blacks and coloreds from whites. Laws prohibiting marriage between races similarly found replication in other states and countries.

The trauma that people of African lineage experienced as their rights were systematically removed bore an eerie connection to the exhibition "Lawyers without Rights," which launched at the University of New Mexico Law School in February, 2017. Close to two hundred attendees crowded into the UNM Law School forum to read poster panels sharing stories of Jewish lawyers who lost their rights to practice law. In towns such as Berlin, sweeping rules disbarred half of the attorney population with no advance notices. Both Jewish and gentile German citizens lost access to representatives in courts. Some attorneys and their clients also lost their lives, as the Nazis transitioned from encouraging Jews to leave Germany to enacting the Final Solution to exterminate those remaining.[2]

Having made prior visits to Germany and the Neuengamme concentration camp in a suburb just outside of Hamburg, I was horrified by this tale of humans' inhumanity toward other humans. At Neuengamme, the Nazis tested the gas that would primarily be used in Poland and other countries to exterminate Jews. The Nazis did not wish to alarm the nearby German populations with the horrid smell accompanying the incineration of colossal numbers of human bodies.

Thoughts about my prior visits to Germany resurfaced after I stumbled upon census records linking my family to people of African origin freed before the Civil War. As my research progressed, I noticed the definitions of "Negro" seemed eerily similar to the definitions of "Jew" in Nazi Germany. In 1785, Virginia defined a Negro as a person who had at least one grandparent who was Negro. The Nazis' Nuremberg Law of 1935, defining who is a Jew, is depicted in Table 12-1. Notice the references to grandparents to determine who is a quarter, half, and full Jew. The consequences for individuals changed with the increasing quantum of Jewish blood.

TABLE 12-1. Legal Definitions of Jews

Legal Definitions	Ancestry Requirement	Consequences
Nuremberg Law of 1935	Prove Aryan Ancestry back to 1750	
Mischling Second Degree (Quarter Jew)	Anyone with one Jewish grandparent	Only permitted to marry Germans.
Mischling (Cross breed in German) First Degree (Half Jew)	Two Jewish grandparents, may also belong to the Jewish religion, or have married a Jew	Could retain citizenship if they converted to Christianity. Excluded from membership in the Nazi Party; drafted in the military; no officers; some incarcerated in concentration camps and deported to death camps

Full Jew	Descended from three or four grandparents	Reich Citizenship Law abolished German citizenship for Jews. In 1938, Jews had to register businesses, wealth and property. They also had to add either "Israel" or "Sara" to their given names, and were prohibited from owning guns. Nazis stamped "J" in their passports. In 1939, Nazi's evicted Jews from their homes.

A quarter Jew (someone with only one Jewish grandparent) was required to marry only Germans. The goal was full assimilation and potentially the production of children who bore only limited traces of their Jewish heritage (similar to the children of Thomas Jefferson and Sally Hemings). This category may have included the Austrian-born Hitler who allegedly had a Jewish grandmother. A half-Jew, which included someone with two Jewish grandparents, or who had married a Jew, or who practiced Judaism, could retain German citizenship if willing to convert to Christianity. Some might find it startling to know that the Nazis classified someone as half Jewish simply for having married a Jew or having converted to Judaism. Some half Jews were deported to death camps. Full Jews (with three or four Jewish grandparents) were designated with yellow stars on their clothing and with "J" stamped in their passports. In 1939, they were evicted from their homes.

While these legal similarities between defining who was a Negro in Virginia and who was a Jew in Germany may astonish, what is perhaps less well known is that the Nazis held a conference during which they deliberately debated modelling their Jewish laws on how Blacks were treated in the southern United States. In his book, *Hitler's American Model: The United States and the Making of Nazi Race Law*, Professor James Q. Whitman documented that the Nazis used United States race laws as a blueprint to create their laws defining who is a Jew.[3] In *Mein Kampf*, Professor Whitman noted, "Hitler praised America as nothing less than 'the one state' that had made progress toward the creation of a healthy racist order."[4] Indeed, two southern historians considered the 1930s Nazi Germany and the American South as a "mirror image."[5]

Another interesting historical parallel with Free Blacks in Virginia developed after the Nazis encouraged Jews to leave Germany. A century earlier, Free Blacks had been encouraged to leave Virginia, only to have neighboring states pass laws forbidding Free Blacks from settling in their territories. Several European countries reacted by passing laws prohibiting the emigration of Jews into their territories. Switzerland passed the Laws of Foreigners to prevent Jews from relocating to Switzerland. Even though France had a Jewish prime minister (Léon Blum), the government restricted the influx of Jews.

Across the Atlantic Ocean, the United States initially approved visas for 7,000 Jewish refugees in 1936 and increased that number to 20,000 by 1938. Later that year, however, an opinion poll revealed that 82% of Americans were opposed to admitting large number of Jews. The next year, the United States refused to admit 20,000 Jewish children.

Finally, in all stories of societies whose morals diverge from honoring humanity, there are always tales of those who helped the threatened. The stories of Schindler's list and Anne Frank's protectors are well known. As indicated by some of the petitions within Virginia there were whites who stood up for their neighbors in courts to protect black neighbors from having their property confiscated or from being evicted from the state.

Moreover, many white Virginians decided after the Revolutionary War that they could no longer keep Africans in bondage when they had just successfully fought to liberate themselves from a foreign oppressor. Many previously unknown men, like Amelia County planter Benjamin Crawley, liberated dozens of their slaves, including Gideon "Geddy" Hill. Other famous men, like George Washington, sought to set an example for others by freeing men and women held in bondage through their last wills.

Lamentably, horrible laws reproduced themselves with dire consequences for unfortunate victims. The Nazis' Final Solution evolved after other countries refused to take Jews. Free Blacks, like Sarah Spears who willed her husband Bob to their children to keep him safe, engaged in strange machinations to protect loved ones who could not safely emigrate from Virginia. After the conclusion of World War II, many German Jews migrated to Israel, seeking solace and freedom from persecution. Similarly, Free Blacks had migrated to Liberia before the Civil War.

* * * * *

Similar replication occurred in South Africa during the time of Apartheid when White South Africans defined Africans as less than other and began to copy the nineteenth century American Jim Crow laws. The South African Senate and House of Assembly passed the Immorality Act in 1927 to "prohibit illicit carnal inter-course between Europeans and natives."[6] Its provisions threatened imprisonment for up to five years for men who had "illicit carnal intercourse" with women from a different race and women with up to four years of imprisonment for having "illicit carnal intercourse," with men from a different race.[7]

South Africa's 1950 Population Registration Act banned mar-riages and sex between blacks and whites. Such a ban led come-dian Trevor Noah to write the book *Born a Crime*,[8] since he was the product of sex between his African mother and Swiss-German Father. Noah's Swiss-German father was from the German-speak-ing section of Switzerland, primarily associated with Zurich and its surrounding areas.

Similar to laws passed in Virginia and Nazi Germany, South Af-rica enacted laws defining whites (Europeans), blacks (Africans), and colored (persons who were the product of two or more races or neither white nor black). Indians, Pakistanis and Japanese, for example were classified as coloreds. Whites were given the most privileges of citizenship, the colored were granted an intermediate level of civil liberties, and blacks received the least amount of legal rights. These distinctions are depicted in Table 12-2.

The pencil test was used to distinguish the lighter skinned from

TABLE 12-2. Apartheid South Africa Definition of
Black and Colored

Classifications	Racial Heritage	How Determined	Level of Privileges
Blacks	African (Bantu)	By Sight	Restricted Rights
Colored	Mixed Race, Indians, Pakistanis, Japanese	Pencil Test	Intermediate Civil Liberties
White	English, Dutch, or other European	By Sight	Full Citizenship Privileges

their darker skinned neighbors. The South African authorities in-
serted a pencil into a person's hair. If the writing instrument stayed
in, the person was classified as black; if it fell out, the person was
deemed a colored. The legal definition of a white person was someone who appeared white. The Population Registration Act of 1950
defined a white person living under apartheid as "one who in ap-
pearance is obviously white."[9]

South Africa's race classifications affected education, employment, housing, transportation, property ownership, sports, voting, and every form of human interaction. The Pass Law required
blacks to register, and carry passes at all times, similar to Virginia's
registry system for Free Blacks. The Group Areas Act, for example,
mandated that people be separated and housed according to race.
The Truth and Reconciliation Commission said about the Act, "in
human terms, the consequences was immense suffering and huge
losses of property and income."[10] Although the Act was abolished a
few years before the end of Apartheid and the transition to demo-
cratic rule in 1994, I observed the continuing consequences during
a 2000 visit to lecture at the University of the Western Cape.

In Capetown, whites lived in mansion-like buildings or elegant
condos, in sections of the city whose beauty rivaled that of Paris or
San Francisco. Coloreds lived in moderate three bedroom, two bath-

room homes, while the majority black population dwelled in shanty towns. See Figure 12-3 for an example of housing for coloreds that I photographed in 2000 while visiting Capetown, South Africa.

Figure 12-3: Housing for Coloreds in South Africa

As you can see, the housing for coloreds was modest housing for a middle class person that might be found in contemporary United States.

By contrast, see Figure 12-4 for an example of housing for South African blacks that I also photographed in 2000 while visiting Capetown, South Africa. These self-made shacks were constructed from tin, corrugated iron, wood, or anything else available nearby. For

Figure 12-4: Housing for Blacks in South Africa

electricity, blacks self-wired their homes by tapping into nearby power lines. The structures had no running water or sewage pick-up in 2000, although the democratically elected government was working hard to correct theses disparities.

* * * * *

Social movements destroyed legal aspects of racial discrimination in Apartheid South Africa, and wars liberated Jews in Europe and blacks from slavery in the United States. Yet, the story replication of countries defining others as "less than" continues. Currently, millions of refugees are persecuted in the countries of their births and seek asylum elsewhere. Starting in 2017, the United States government implemented policies separating children from their parents at the southern border with Mexico. The horrific images of crying infants seemed eerily reminiscent of what enslaved blacks suffered in the South when children were torn from their mothers at the auction block or on a plantation to be sold.

After the images of crying-separated children brought some shame to the administration, it reunited some, but not all, the families. Eventually, the administration acknowledged that some children could not be reunited with their parents because of inadequate paperwork. Thus, some of these children could share the fate of enslaved babies who never saw their mothers and fathers again. However, this seems an odd resignation to bad circumstances when the advancement of technology should permit the reunification of families with DNA testing. During the era of Reconstruction, many newly emancipated slaves viewed their liberation as "incomplete until the families which had been dispersed by slavery were reunited."[11] Separated migrant families should not have to endure the same fate.

The migrants' plight recalls the often repeated mantra that history is like an art gallery with few originals and many reproductions. Societies have replicated horrific racial interactions, often to the detriment of those with darker skin. If people truly understood their history, they might harbor less animosity toward others. People could easily contain within their own DNA a segment of those groups they seek to exclude.

History has written multiple scripts with the same themes and different characters. While what happened cannot be altered, citizens can learn about the experiences of the Free Blacks of Virginia and other groups to diminish the chances of repeating the mistakes of antiquity.

Sherri Burr
Albuquerque, New Mexico

Acknowledgments

Any book benefits from the assistance of individuals other than the author. I thank my Carolina Academic Press Publisher, Keith Sipe, and his remarkable team that includes Linda Lacy, Jennifer Hill, Tasha Gervais, and Ryland Bowman. I am grateful to Judith Avila and David Steinberg for copy-editing this book. They proved that there can never be enough pairs of eyes reading the same text.

At the University of New Mexico Law School, I will be forever grateful to my assistant Cheryl Burbank, a genealogy researcher and a helpful proofreader, as well as to retired secretary Mary Dewey, retired Library staffer Robert Flinkman, and former dean David Herring who provided two research grants to support the project. Professor Quiche Suzuki read six chapters and provided keen-eyed proofreading comments, and so did several other faculty colleagues, including Ted Parnall, Robert Schwartz, Jennifer Moore and Josh Katzenberg. Michael Norwood gifted me his father's books on American history. Brandon Ilgen, a descendant of John Punch and a member of the University of New Mexico Law School Class of 2019, emailed his family tree on November 15, 2018. The document linked him and President Barack Obama to John Punch whose attempt at self-liberation was punished in 1640 with a lifetime of servitude for running away from his indentured service to a master.

My visit to the Family History Library in Salt Lake City sparked the launch of this project. My travels to the Library of Virginia in Richmond led to meeting librarians Tom Crew and Chris (whose last name I do not remember). I took a class from them, and Chris helped me locate the deed freeing Gideon "Geddy" Hill, my fourth great-grandfather, when he was two years old. My delight when I read this document was immense. When my research seemed to reach a dead-end, Chris suggested that I determine the white family connected to my family and research them. At first I felt shocked to receive such a suggestion, but then I started researching Benjamin Crawley, an amazingly independent man, who by some accounts may have been a minister, a role that Gideon Hill assumed later in life. That Ben Crawley freed fifty people in the 1787 deed most likely altered my family's fortunes for generations, creating at least eight generations of homeowners and counting.

Crawley also eventually freed Suckey, his lover, and their child Jonathan. Despite the restrictions against inter-racial marriage, Crawley married Suckey and left her and his son Jonathan his immense wealth. Suckey was a mulatto, making Jonathan at least three-quarters, and possibly even more, white. He eventually migrated to Missouri where he integrated into white society. When my assistant Cheryl Burbank tracked down some of Jonathan Crawley's modern-day descendants in Missouri, they denied knowing that their ancestor had any trace of African blood.

In Petersburg, Virginia, I am grateful for the time that Julian Green, the First Baptist Church Historian, and Reverend Tillman granted me. First Baptist Church is one of the oldest religious establishments primarily serving African Americans in the Nation. It may be the only church where its pulpit was graced with the sermons of Nat Turner and Dr. Martin Luther King, Junior. At Gillfield Baptist Church, where Gideon Hill, his wife Cecila, and their children worshiped, I benefited from many conversations with Dr. Grady Powell, a Gillfield Historian and Former Pastor. Also in Petersburg, I conversed with Rhonda Gregory, of the Petersburg Circuit Court.

My University of New Mexico colleague Virginia Scharf first suggested that I become acquainted with the Robert H. Smith International Center for Jefferson Studies, which provided me a Monticello Fellowship that enabled me to live in Virginia and research this book. At the Center, I am grateful to the following: Andrew

O'Shaughnessy (the Saunders Director), Anna Berkes (Research Librarian), Christa Dierksheide (Historian), James Hrdlicka (University of Virginia Dissertation Fellow), Jobie Hill (Archaeologist), Endrina Tay (Associate Foundation Librarian for Technical Services), Gaye Wilson (Shannon Senior Historian), Jack Robertson (Foundation Librarian), Kate McDonald (Executive Assistant & Program Administrator), Cinder Stanton (Shannon Senior Historian Emeritus), Tasha Stanton (Executive Assistant & Program Administrator), and Wil Verhoeven (ICJS Fellow and Professor of American Culture and Cultural Theory and Chair of the American Studies Department at Groningen University, the Netherlands). I benefitted from many conversations and the opportunity to bounce off ideas about my research with these individuals.

At the University of Virginia, I appreciate that a coauthor of my Intellectual Property book, Professor Edward Kitch, immediately invited me to dinner and to participate in events at the university founded by Thomas Jefferson.

The Virginia State University Archives provided another treasure trove of material for my research. Fracine Archer and Ronnika Davis provided guidance as I spent hours rummaging through the papers of noted historian Luther Porter Jackson and finding many wonderful stories of Free Blacks to enrich my manuscript.

I am grateful for the support of my family and friends during this long journey. My brother's nearly eight-years in a semi-comatose condition inspired the search for more relatives. My mother has been supportive as I have had to postpone outings with her to write. My nephew travelled with me to England while I spent time in the British Library and the British Archives searching for material about King James I, the Virginia Company and other information on the founding of Jamestown. I am fortunate to have received feedback on various chapters from members of Southwest Writers, the Intrepids, the Mighty Musers, First Fridays, and the Aaron Burr Association.

Bibliography

Baptist, Edward E. *The Half Has Never Been Told: Slavery and the Making of American Capitalism*. New York: Basic Books, 2014

Baumeister, Roy F. and John Tierney. *Willpower: Rediscovering the Greatest Human Strength*. New York: The Penguin Press, 2011

Berlin, Ira. *Slaves without Masters: The Free Negro in the Antebellum South*. New York: The New Press, 1974.

Boles, John B. *Jefferson: Architect of American Liberty*. New York: Basic Books, 2017.

Brands, H.W. *The First American: The Life and Times of Benjamin Franklin*. New York: Anchor Books, 2000.

Breen, T.H. and Stephen Innes. *Myne Owne Ground: Race and Freedom on Virginia's Eastern Shore, 1640–1676* (25th Ann. Ed., 2005). New York: Oxford University Press, 2005.

Brodie, Fawn M., *Thomas Jefferson: An Intimate History*. New York: Norton, 1974.

Burr, Sherri. "Defining Others to Justify Abolishing Legal and Human Rights: Parallels between Jews in Nazi Germany and Free Blacks in Colonial Virginia," in 31, No. 4 *New Mexico Jewish Historical Society Legacy* (Winter 2017–2018).

Burr, Sherri, "The Free Blacks of Virginia: A Personal Narrative, A Legal Construct," 19, No. 1 *The Iowa Journal of Gender, Race & Justice* 1 (Spring 2016).

Cesarani, David. *Final Solution: The Fate of the Jews 1933–1949*. New York: St. Martin's Press, 2016.

Charles, Patrick. *Washington's Decision: The Story of George Washington's Decision to Reaccept Black Enlistments in the Continental Army, December 31, 1775*. Book Surge (now Create Space), 2005.

Chernow, Ron. *Alexander Hamilton*. New York: Penguin Books, 2004.

Chernow, Ron. *Grant*. New York: Penguin Press, 2017.

Dierksheide, Christa. *Amelioration and Empire: Progress and Slavery in the Plantation Americas*. Charlottesville: The University of Virginia Press, 2014.

Dunbar, Erica Armstrong. *Never Caught: The Washingtons' Relentless Pursuit of Their Runaway Slave Ona Judge*. New York, Atria, 2017.

Ellis, Joseph J. *Founding Brothers: The Revolutionary Generation*. New York: Vintage Books, 2000, 2002.

Ellis, Joseph. *His Excellency George Washington*. New York: Alfred A. Knopf, 2004.

Foner, Eric. *Forever Free: The Story of Emancipation & Reconstruction*. New York: Vintage Books, 2005.

Franklin, Benjamin. *The Autobiography of Benjamin Franklin*. Mineola, Dover Publications, Inc., 1996.

Fraser, Antonia. *Mary Queen of Scots*. New York: Dell Publishing, 1969.

Gordon-Reed, Annette. *The Hemingses of Monticello*. New York: Norton, 2008.

Gordon-Reed, Annette. *Thomas Jefferson and Sally Hemings: An American Controversy*. Charlottesville: University of Virginia Press, 1997.

Gordon-Reed, Annette, and Peter S. Onuf. "*Most Blessed of the Patriarchs*": *Thomas Jefferson and the Empire of the Imagination*. New York: W.W. Norton & Company, 2016.

Grant, Ulysses S. *Personal Memoirs of U.S. Grant*. Cambridge: Da Capo Press, 2001.

Guild, June Purcell. *Black Laws of Virginia*. Westminster: Heritage Books, 1995, 2011 (Originally published in 1936 by Whittet & Shepperson).

Heinegg, Paul. *Free African Americans of North Carolina, Virginia, and South Carolina: From the Colonial Period to About 1820*, 5th Ed. Baltimore: Clearfield Company, 2005.

Higginbotham, A. Leon. *In the Matter of Color: Race and the American Legal Process, The Colonial Period*. New York: Oxford University Press, 1978.

Higginbotham, A. Leon and Bosworth, Greer C. "'Rather Than the Free': Free Blacks in Colonial and Antebellum Virginia." 26 *Harv. C.R.-Civ. Liberties L. Rev.* 30 (1991).

Hoffer, Peter Charles. *The Treason Trials of Aaron Burr.* Lawrence: University Press of Kansas, 2008.

Hurston, Zora Neale. *Barracoon: The Story of the Last "Black Cargo."* New York: Amistad, 2018.

Isaacson, Walter. *Benjamin Franklin: An American Life.* New York: Simon & Schuster, 2003.

Isenberg, Nancy. *Fallen Founder: The Life of Aaron Burr.* New York: Penguin Books, 2007.

Jackson, Luther Porter. *A Short History of the Gillfield Baptist Church of Petersburg, VA.*

Jackson, Luther Porter. *Free Negro Labor & Property Holding in Virginia, 1830–1860.* New York: Athenum, 1969.

Jacobs, Harriet. *Incidents in the Life of a Slave Girl.* Mineola: Dover Publications, 2001 (Originally published in 1861).

Jefferson, Thomas. *Notes on the State of Virginia* (1785)Memphis: General Books LLC, 2012.

Katz, Ellen D. "African- American Freedom in Antebellum Cumberland County, Virginia," 70 Chi.- Kent L. Rev. 1995.

Keckley, Elizabeth. *Behind the Scenes. Or, Thirty Years a Slave, and Four Years in the White House.* New York: Oxford University Press, 1988.

Lebsock, Suzanne. *The Free Women of Petersburgh: Status and Culture in a Southern Town, 1784–1860.* New York: W.W. Norton & Company, 1984.

Madden, Jr., T. O. *We Were Always Free: The Maddens of Culpeper County, Virginia: A 200–Year Family History.* Charlottesville: University of Virginia Press, 1992.

Maris-Wolf, Ted. *Family Bonds: Free Blacks and Re-enslavement Law in Antebellum Virginia.* Chapel Hill: The University of North Carolina Press, 2015.

McCullough, David. *John Adams.* New York: Simon & Schuster, 2001.

McCullough, David. *1776.* New York: Simon & Schuster, 2005.

Miller, John Chester. *The Wolf by the Ears: Thomas Jefferson and Slavery.* Charlottesville: The University Press of Virginia, 1991.

Noah, Trevor. *Born a Crime.* New York: Penguin, Random House, 2016.

Northup, Solomon. *12 Years a Slave*. New York, Penguin Books, 2013 (First Published in the United States by Derby and Miller, 1853).

O'Shaughnessy, Andrew Jackson. *The Men Who Lost America: British Leadership, the American Revolution and the Fate of the Empire*. New Haven: Yale University Press, 2013.

Price, David A. *Love and Hate in Jamestown: John Smith, Pocahontas and the Heart of a New Nation*. London: Faber and Faber Limited, 2003.

Reynolds, David S. *John Brown, Abolitionist: The Man Who Killed Slavery, Sparked the Civil War, and Seeded Civil Rights*. New York: Alfred A. Knopf, 2005.

Rothman, Joshua. *Notorious in the Neighborhood: Sex and Families Across the Color Line in Virginia, 1787–1861*. Chapel Hill: The University of North Carolina Press, 2003.

Russell, John H. *The Free Negro in Virginia*, 1619–1865. Baltimore: The Johns Hopkins Press, 1913.

Scharff, Virginia. *The Women Jefferson Loved*. New York: Harper-Collins, 2010.

Scott, Otto J. *James I*. New York: Mason/Charter, 1976.

Stahr, Walter. *John Jay: Founding Father*. London: Hambledon and London, 2005.

Stanton, Lucia. *Those Who Labor for My Happiness: Slavery at Thomas Jefferson's Monticello*. Charlottesville: The University of Virginia Press, 2012.

The Writers' Program of the Work Projects Admin. in the State of Va. *The Negro in Virginia*. Winston-Salem: John F. Blair, Publisher,1940.

Von Daacke, Kirt. *Freedom has a Face: Race, Identity, and Community in Jefferson's Virginia*. Charlottesville: University of Virginia Press, 2012.

Washington, Booker T. *Up From Slavery*. New York: Penguin Books, 1901, 1986.

Webb, Frank J. *The Garies and Their Friends*. London: G. Routledge & Co., 1857.

Notes

Author's Note

1. Some of the material in this introductory note and throughout the book was originally printed in the article by Sherri Burr, *The Free Blacks of Virginia: A Personal Narrative, A Legal Construct*, 19 The Journal of Gender, Race & Justice 1 (Spring 2016). In this book, I have freely used my own words first in that University of Iowa College of Law Journal without additional citation.

2. Personal details for George W. Hill in household of Gideon Hill, United States Census, 1850. *Available at* https://familysearch.org (On file with the Author).

3. The author capitalizes "Free Black" or "Free Blacks" throughout this book to refer to the unique class of people of African descent who were either never in bondage or were liberated before the Civil War. The author does not capitalize generalized references to blacks or whites, although they refer to a group, unless either word starts a sentence.

Introduction

1. This introduction uses narrative nonfiction techniques. The dialogue has been created for dramatic effect and to clarify arcane language in court and tribunal records. The information originally available has been cited in these notes. Since the first recording device was not invented until 1876, it is impossible to know exactly what people said.

2. In their book, "*Myne Owne Ground*": *Race and Freedom on Virginia's Eastern Shore, 1640–1676*, T.H. Breen and Stephen Innes wrote that these events took place when Captain Gouldsmith visited Anthony Johnson's

plantation. They also wrote that "Robert Parker and his brother George took Casor's side in the dispute," but do not state when or where that happened. See T.H. Breen and Stephen Innes , *"Myne Owne Ground": Race and Freedom on Virginia's Eastern Shore, 1640–1676*, (New York: Oxford University Press, 1980), 13. (25th Anniversary Edition, 2005, also available).

3. John Russell, *The Free Negro in Virginia, 1619–1865* (Baltimore: The John Hopkins Press, 1913), 88 ("Among the early Virginia land patents were a number representing grants to negroes of from fifty to five hundred acres to be held in fee simple. The first of such grants made to a [N]egro of which we have any record was one of two hundred and fifty acres to Anthony Johnson of Northampton County in 1651 as "head-rights" on the importation of five persons into the colony.").

4. *Ibid.*, 32–33. The prologue is taken from this description of what happened in the unusual case. Its language has been modernized for current sensitivities. "According to the records made of the situation, John Casor set up the claim in 1653 'Yt hee came unto Virginia for seaven or eight years of Indenture, yt hee had demanded his freedom of Anth. Johnson his Mayster; & further sd yt hee had kept him his serv[an]t seaven years longer than hee should or ought.' Casor appealed to Captain Samuel Goldsmith to see that he was accorded his rights. Goldsmith demanded of Johnson the servant negro's indenture, and was told by Johnson that the latter had never seen any indenture, and 'yt hee had ye Negro for his life.' Casor stood firmly by his assertion that when he came in he had an indenture, and Messrs. Robert and George Parker confirmed his declaration, saying that "they knewe that ye sd Negro had an Indenture in one Mr. [Sandys] hand, on ye other side of ye Baye & . . . if the sd Anth. Johnson did not let ye negro go free the said negro Jno. Casor would recover most of his Cows from him ye sd Johnson" in compensation for service rendered which was not due. Whereupon Anthony Johnson "was in great feare," and his "sonne in Law, his wife, & his own two sonnes persuaded the old negro Anth. Johnson to set the sd Jno. Casor free."

5. David A. Price, *Love and Hate in Jamestown: John Smith, Pocahontas and the Heart of a New Nation* (New York: Knopf, 2003), 218.

6. Russell, *The Free Negro, supra* note 3, 32–33.

7. *Ibid.*

8. *Ibid.*

9. *Ibid.*

10. *Ibid.*

11. *Ibid.*

12. *Ibid.*

13. *Ibid.*

14. *Ibid.*, 24, FN 34.

15. Breen and Innes, *supra* note 5, 10. "Mary bore Anthony at least four children, and still managed to outlive her husband by several years. In a society in which marriages were routinely broken by early death, Mary and Anthony lived together for over forty years."

16. Russell, *supra* note 3, 32–33.

17. *Ibid.*

18. *Ibid.*

19. *Ibid.*

20. *Ibid.*

21. *Ibid.*

22. *Ibid.*, 24. ("Among the twenty-three African "servants" enumerated in 1624 was a Negro man named Anthony.")

Chapter One

1. T.H. Breen and Stephen Innes, *"Myne Owne Ground": Race and Freedom on Virginia's Eastern Shore, 1640–1676* (New York: Oxford Press, 1980, 2005), 8: "Johnson arrived in Virginia sometime in 1621 aboard the *James*. People referred to him at this time simply as 'Antonio a Negro.'"

2. *Encyclopedia Britannica online*, s.v., *Ndongo/historical kingdom, Africa,* available at Britannica.com. Last visited 7/13/2016.

3. *Encyclopedia Britannica online*, s.v., *Ndongo/historical kingdom, Africa,* available at Britannica.com. Last visited 7/13/2016. See also Country Studies, "Angola-Ndongo Kingdom," available at http://countrystudies.us/angola/6.htm, accessed July 12, 2016). Some sources spell these river names as Kwanza and Lukala. *See* Wikipedia, "Slavery in Angola," https://en.wikipedia.org/wikiSlavery_in_Angola.

4. *Angola: A Country Study*, 8.

5. David A. Price, *Love and Hate in Jamestown: John Smith, Pocahontas and the Heart of a New Nation* (New York: Knopf, 2003), 196.

6. The original spelling of the colony was Jamestowne, with an "e" on the end. For the purposes of this book, the author has chosen to spell it

Jamestown. The colony was named after King James 1 of England, who as James VI of Scotland had inherited England after the death of his barren cousin, Elizabeth I. He also provided the name for the *King James Bible*.

7. Olaudah Equiano, "The Interesting Narrative of the Life of Olaudah Equiano, or Gusavus Vassa, The African," in *The Classic Slave Narratives*, ed. Henry Louis Gates, Jr. (New York: Signet Classic, 2012), 47.

8. *Ibid.*

9. *Ibid.*

10. *Ibid.*, 48.

11. *Ibid.*, 54.

12. Murphy, *History of African Civilization: The peoples, nations, kingdoms and empires of Africa from prehistory to the present* (New York: Thomas Y. Crowell Co., 1972), 270.

13. Eric Foner, *Forever Free: The Story of Emancipation & Reconstruction* (New York: Vintage Books, 2005), 14.

14. Murphy, *supra* note 12, 287.

15. *Ibid.*

16. *Ibid.*, 288.

17. *Ibid.*

18. *Ibid.*, 263–264.

19. *Ibid.*, 264.

20. *Ibid.*

21. While we do not know the exact circumstances of Anthony "Antonio" Johnson's kidnapping, this is a plausible inference from the historical records. The author visited recreated ships in Jamestown to obtain an idea of what the Atlantic Ocean voyage could have been like for African captives.

22. Gerald F. Bender, *Angola under the Portuguese: The Myth and the Reality* (Berkeley: Univ. of Calif. Press, 1978), 60.

23. *Ibid.*

Chapter Two

1. Olaudah Equiano, "The Interesting Narrative of the Life of Olaudah Equiano, or Gusavus Vassa, The African," in *The Classic Slave Narratives*, ed. Henry Louis Gates, Jr. (New York: Signet Classic, 2012), 48.

2. Recreated ships can be seen at the recreated Jamestown Settlement in Virginia.

3. Equiano, *supra* note 1, 57.

4. As will be discussed in the chapter on Virginia, some Portuguese and Spanish ships were intercepted and had their cargo captured with no shots fired. Captains Jope and Elfrith who took control of the *São Joao Bāutista* off the coast of Mexico without firing a shot exemplified these kinds of ship leaders. *See* David A. Price, *Love and Hate in Jamestown: John Smith, Pocahontas and the Heart of a New Nation* (New York: Knopf, 2003), 195.

5. T.H. Breen and Stephen Innes, *"Myne Owne Ground": Race and Freedom on Virginia's Eastern Shore, 1640–1676* (New York: Oxford Press, 1980, 2005), 8: "Johnson arrived in Virginia sometime in 1621 aboard the *James*. People referred to him at this time simply as 'Antonio a Negro.'"

6. Zora Neale Hurston, *Barracoon: The Story of the Last "Black Cargo"* (New York: Amistad, 2018), xxviv.

Chapter Three

1. These cargo ships have been recreated and can be viewed at the modern-day Jamestown Visitor Center in Virginia.

2. David A. Price, *Love and Hate in Jamestown: John Smith, Pocahontas and the Heart of a New Nation* (New York: Knopf, 2003), 16.

3. Otto J. Scott, *James I* (New York: Mason/Charter, 1976), 260.

4. Visitors to Edinburgh Palace can stand in the actual alcove where James I was born in 1556, just as the author did in September 2017, and wrote about in an article "The Writing Life: Researching James I/VI," *Southwest Sage*, November 2017.

5. Antonia Fraser, *Mary Queen of Scots* (New York: Dell Publishing, 1969), 458.

6. Scott, *supra* note 3, 9.

7. *Ibid.*, 353.

8. Price, *supra* note 2, 33–34.

9. *Ibid.*, 35.

10. Niraj Chokshi, "Before Global Warming, Humans Caused Global Cooling, Study Finds," *New York Times* (Feb. 5, 2019).

11. *Ibid.*

12. *Ibid.*

13. Price, *supra* note 2, 38.

14. *Ibid.*, 127.

15. *Ibid.*, 129.

16. *Ibid.*, 195.

17. *Ibid.*, 196.

18. *Ibid.*, 196–197.

19. *Ibid.*, 197.

20. *Ibid.*

21. A. Leon Higginbotham , *In the Matter of Color: Race and the American Legal Process: The Colonial Period* (New York, Oxford University Press, 1978), 19.

22. Price, *supra* note 2, 197–198.

23. *Ibid.*, 198.

24. *Ibid.*, 6–7.

25. *Ibid.*, 7.

26. T.H. Breen and Stephen Innes, *"Myne Owne Ground": Race and Freedom on Virginia's Eastern Shore, 1640–1676* (New York: Oxford Press, 1980, 2005), 8.

27. *Ibid.*, 9.

28. Price, *supra* note 2, 186.

29. *Ibid.*, 196.

30. *Ibid.*

31. Breen and Innes, *supra* note 26, 9–10.

32. *Ibid.*, 9.

33. *Ibid.*, 9–10.

34. *Ibid.*

35. *Ibid.*, 10.

36. John Russell, *The Free Negro in Virginia, 1619–1865* (Baltimore: The John Hopkins Press, 1913), 23.

37. *Ibid.*, 24.

38. *Ibid.*, 18.

Chapter Four

1. June Purcell Guild, *Black Laws of Virginia* (1936) (Westminster: Heritage Books, 1995, 2011), 37.

2. John Russell, *The Free Negro in Virginia, 1619–1865* (Baltimore: The John Hopkins Press, 1913), 23.

3. Daphne Gentry, Headrights (VA-NOTES*)*, Richmond, VA: Library of Virginia), Accessed Oct. 12, 2015, http://www.lva.virginia.gov/public/guides/va4_headrights.htm.

4. *Ibid.*

5. *Ibid.*

6. The Writers' Program of the Work Projects Admin. in the State of Va., *The Negro in Virginia* (Winston-Salem: John F. Blair, Publisher, 1940), 5.

7. Russell, *supra* note 2, 25.

8. *Ibid.*

9. Charles Perdue, foreword to *The Negro in Virginia* by The Writer's Program of the Work Projects Admin. in the State of Va. (1940), vii–ix. The Writer's Program of the Work Projects Administration in the State of Virginia was established in the midst of the Great Depression to put unemployed professionals to work. Their book contained ex-slave interviews.

10. The Writers' Program *supra* note 6.

11. *Ibid.*

12. Thomas Collelo, ed., *Angola: A Country Study* (Library of Congress, Fed. Research Div., 3rd ed., 1989), 5 ("The Bantu speakers were a negroid people, adept at farming, hunting, and gathering.")

13. T.H. Breen and Stephen Innes, *"Myne Owne Ground": Race and Freedom on Virginia's Eastern Shore, 1640–1676* (New York: Oxford Press, 1980, 2005), 71.

14. *Ibid.*, 25–26; Guild, *supra* note 1, 37.

15. Breen and Innes, *supra* note 13, 26.

16. A. Leon Higginbotham, *In the Matter of Color: Race and the American Legal Process: The Colonial Period* (New York: Oxford University Press, 1978), 58.

17. *Ibid.*, 26.

18. *Ibid.*, 27.

19. *Ibid.*

20. *Ibid.*

21. *Ibid.*, 28.

22. *Ibid.*

23. John Punch → John Bunch I → John Bunch II → John Bunch III → Samuel Bunch → Charles Bunch → Nathanial Bunch → Anna Bunch → Frances Allred → Margaret Wright → Leona McCurry → Madelyn Payne → Stanley Ann Dunham → Barack Obama. Many thanks to Brandon Ilgen, a descendant of John Punch and a member of the University of New Mexico Law School Class of 2019, for giving me this family tree on November 15, 2018. The tree remains on file with the author.

24. Breen and Innes, *supra* note 13, 82–83.

25. *Ibid.*, 11.

26. Russell, *supra* note 2, 25.

27. Breen and Innes, *supra* note 13, 11.

28. Luther Porter Jackson, *Rights and Duties in A Democracy* (August 14, 1946) (Available in the Special Collections/Archives in Virginia State University's Johnston Memorial Library).

29. *Ibid.*

30. *Ibid.*

31. Russell, *supra* note 2, 24. "In the county court records of Northampton, of date February 28, 1652, is the following order: "Upon ye humble pet[ition[of Anth. Johnson Negro; & Mary his wife; & their Information to ye Court that they have been Inhabitants of Virginia above thirty years consideration being taken of their hard labor & honoured service performed by the petitioners in this County, for ye obtayneing of their Livelyhood And ye great Llosse they have sustained by an unfortunate fire with their present charge to provide for, Be it therefore fitt and ordered that from the day of the date hereof (during their natural lives) the sd Mary Johnson & two daughters of Anthony Johnson Negro be disingaged and freed from payment of Taxes and leaves in Northampton County for public use."

32. Breen and Innes, *supra* note 13, 12.

33. Guild, *supra* note 1, 126. See Act VIII (1644).

34. *Ibid.*, 129. See Act VII (1668).

35. *Ibid.*, 129 (footnote omitted).

36. Russell, *supra* note 2, 32, FN 61.

37. *Ibid.*, 32–33.

38. *Ibid.*, 33.

39. Breen and Innes, *supra* note 13, 17.

Chapter Five

1. John Russell, *The Free Negro in Virginia, 1619–1865* (Baltimore: The John Hopkins Press, 1913), 22.

2. *Ibid.*, 23.

3. *Ibid.*, 24.

4. See www.slavevoyages.org. Accessed February 5, 2019.

5. *Ibid.*

6. June Purcell Guild, *Black Laws of Virginia* (1936) (Westminster: Heritage Books, 1995, 2011), 21.

7. *Ibid.*

8. *Ibid.*

9. *Ibid.*, 21–22.

10. *Ibid.*, 21.

11. *Ibid.*, 22.

12. *Ibid.*

13. *Ibid.*

14. T.H. Breen and Stephen Innes, *"Myne Owne Ground": Race and Freedom on Virginia's Eastern Shore, 1640–1676* (New York: Oxford Press, 1980, 2005), 96.

15. *Ibid.*

16. *Ibid.*

17. *Ibid.*

18. Guild, *supra* note 6, 55–56. (Chapter XIV (1748) providing in part, "Children are to be bond or free, according to the condition of their mother.").

19. *Ibid.*, 23.

20. Russell, *supra* note 1, 37.

21. Guild, *supra* note 6, 23.

22. Rebecca Carroll, "Margaret Garner," *New York Times* (Feb. 3, 2019). The New York Times ran a delayed obituary on Garner on that date.

23. Harriet Jacobs, *Incidents in the Life of a Slave Girl* (Mineola: Dover Publications, 2001) (Originally published in 1861).

24. Russell, *supra* note 1, 22.

25. Guild, *supra* note 6, 24.

26. *Ibid.*

27. *Ibid.*

28. *Ibid.*, 24–25.

29. Loving v. Virginia, 388 U.S. 1 (1967).

30. See references to Mark Twains' *The Adventures of Tom Sawyer* reprinted in Roy F. Baumeister and John Tierney, *Willpower: Rediscovering the Greatest Human Strength* (New York: The Penguin Press, 2011), 234.

31. Meghan Carr Horrigan, "The State of Marriage in Virginia History: A Legislative Means of Identifying the Cultural Other," 9 *Georgetown Journal of Gender and Law* 9, no 1 (2008): 379, 383.

32. *Ibid.*

Chapter Six

1. A. Leon Higginbotham, *In the Matter of Color: Race and the American Legal Process, The Colonial Period* (New York, Oxford University Pres, 1978), 21.

2. T.H. Breen and Stephen Innes, *"Myne Owne Ground": Race and Freedom on Virginia's Eastern Shore, 1640–1676* (New York: Oxford Press, 1980, 2005), 107–108.

3. John Russell, *The Free Negro in Virginia, 1619–1865* (Baltimore: The John Hopkins Press, 1913), 40–41.

4. June Purcell Guild, *Black Laws of Virginia* (1936) (Westminster: Heritage Books, 1995, 2011).

5. *Ibid.*

6. *Ibid.*, 27.

7. *Ibid.*

8. Act XVI (1691) provided, "Negroes who are set free must be transported out of the county by the person giving them freedom within six months after such setting free." *Ibid.*, 94 (footnote omitted). In 1831, the legislation became harsher. Chapter XXXIX (1831) provided, "Free Negroes and mulattoes who remain in the Commonwealth contrary to law are to be sold publicly." *Ibid.*, 106. Thus, Free Blacks who did not depart Virginia risked re-enslavement.

9. Russell, *supra* note 3, 10. (footnote omitted). *See also*, Guild, *supra* note 4, 47.

10. Guild, *supra* note 4, 47.

11. *Ibid.*

12. Solomon Northup, *12 Years a Slave* (New York: Penguin Books, 2013 (First published in the United States by Derby and Miller, 1853), 169.

13. *Ibid.*

14. *Ibid.*

15. Examples can be found from visiting old plantations that are open for tourist visitations, such as Mount Vernon.

16. Guild, *supra* note 4, 47.

17. *Ibid.*, 41.

18. *Ibid.*, 53.

19. *Ibid.*

20. *Ibid.*, 52.

21. *Ibid.*

22. *Ibid.*, 57.

23. Higginbotham, *supra* note 1, 49.

24. *Ibid.*

25. In 1863, the South was in rebellion so the Proclamation did not become effective until after they had lost the war.

26. Higginbotham, *supra* note 1, 39.

27. *Ibid.*

28. *Ibid.*

29. *Ibid.*

30. *Ibid.*

31. *Ibid.*, 40.

32. Joan W. Peters, *Introduction* to June Purcell Guild, *Black Laws of Virginia* (Westminster: Heritage Books 2011) (First Published in 1936 by Whittet & Shepperson), 130 n.9.

33. Guild, *supra* note 4, 132.

34. The Fifth Amendment was ratified on February 3, 1870. U.S. Const. Amend. XV, § 1.

35. *Ibid.*

36. According to the United States Justice Department website,

[t]he Voting Rights Act, adopted initially in 1965 and extended in 1970, 1975, and 1982, is generally considered the most successful piece of civil rights legislation ever adopted by the United States Congress. The Act codifies and effectuates the 15th Amendment's permanent guarantee that, throughout the nation, no person shall be denied the right to vote on account of race or color. In addition, the Act contains several special provisions that impose even more stringent requirements in certain jurisdictions throughout the country.

Introduction to Federal Voting Rights Laws, U.S. Dep't. of Just., http:// www.justice.gov/crt/about/vot/intro/intro.php (last updated Aug. 6, 2015). In recent years, the Voting Rights Act of 1965 has come under attack. In

2013, for example, the U.S. Supreme Court struck down Section 4(b) on the coverage formula as unconstitutional. *Shelby County v. Holder*, 133 S. Ct. 2612, 2651 (2013). See also, Ari Berman, Ari, *Give Us the Ballot* (New York: Picador Farrar, Straus and Giroux, 2015) (detailing other efforts to unravel the Voting Rights Act).

37. *Introduction to Federal Voting Rights Laws*, U.S. Dep't. of Just., http://www.justice.gov/crt/about/vot/intro/intro.php.

38. *Ibid.*

39. See also, Ari Berman, *Give Us the Ballot* (New York: Picador Farrar, Straus and Giroux, 2015) (detailing other efforts to unravel the Voting Rights Act).

40. Guild, *supra* note 4, 132.

41. *Ibid.*, 129 (footnote omitted). Chapter IV (1723) provided, "All free Negroes, mulattoes, and Indians (except tributary Indians to this government), male and female above sixteen years of age, and all wives of such, shall be deemed tithables." *Ibid.*, 131. This same act removed the right of Free Blacks to vote, by providing, "No free Negro or Indian whatsoever shall hereafter have any vote at any election." *Ibid.*, 132.

42. *Ibid.*, 129.

43. Chapter XXIII (1705) provided, in part,

All Negro, mulatto, and Indian slaves within this dominion shall be held to be real estate and not chattels and shall descend unto heirs and widows according to the custom of land inheritance, and be held in fee simple. Provided that any merchant bringing slaves into this dominion shall hold such slaves whilst they remain unsold as personal estate. All such slaves may be taken on execution as other chattels; slaves shall not be escheatable.

Ibid., 48. The latter phrase references the normal right of the state to take property if heirs cannot be found. Under this provision, the territory of Virginia forfeited the right to receive slaves if heirs could not be found.

44. Chapter II (1748) provided, "Negroes having been declared to be real estate in 1705 and afterward this explained by act in 1727 and the acts having been found inconvenient, they are repealed, and for the future all slaves shall be taken to be chattels." *Ibid.*, 55 (footnote omitted).

45. *Ibid.*,131.

46. *Ibid.*

47. *The Favourite*, Directed by Yorgos Lanthimos (2018).

48. *Mary Queen of Scots,* Directed by Josie Rourke (2018).

49. Guild, *supra* note 4, 48.

50. *Ibid.*

51. John B. Boles, *Jefferson: Architect of American Liberty* (New York: Basic Books, 2017), 454.

52. Harriet Jacobs, *Incidents in the Life of a Slave Girl* (Mineola: Dover Publications, 2001), 10. This book was originally published in 1861, in Boston.

53. Guild, *supra* note 4, 96.

54. *Ibid.*

55. *Ibid.,* 131.

56. *Ibid.,* 55.

57. *The Will of J. John Pinick of the County of Prince Edward* is on file with the author.

58. The Deed book index page 70 referencing *Deed of Gift from John Wallis to Aggatha Stephens, wife of Joseph Stephens* is on file with the author.

59. *Ibid.*

Chapter Seven

1. David McCullough, *John Adams* (New York: Simon & Schuster, 2001), 59.

2. *Ibid.*

3. *Ibid.*

4. *Ibid.*

5. *Ibid.*

6. John B. Boles, *Jefferson: Architect of American Liberty* (New York: Basic Books, 2017), 25.

7. *Ibid.*

8. *Ibid.,* 32.

9. H.W. Brands, *The First American: The Life and Times of Benjamin Franklin* (New York: Anchor Books, 2000), 2.

10. Andrew Jackson O'Shaughnessy, *The Men Who Lost America: British Leadership, the American Revolution and the Fate of the Empire* (New Haven: Yale University Press, 2013), 5.

11. *Ibid.,* Figure 6.

12. McCullough, *John Adams, supra* note 1, 13.

13. A. Leon Higginbotham, *In the Matter of Color: Race and the American Legal Process, The Colonial Period* (New York: Oxford University Press, 1978), 374.

14. O'Shaughnessy, *supra* note 10, 11.

15. David McCullough, *1776* (New York: Simon & Schuster, 2005), 24.

16. Patrick Charles, *Washington's Decision: The Story of George Washington's Decision to Reaccept Black Enlistments in the Continental Army, December 31, 1775* (Book Surge, 2005), 3.

17. *Ibid.*

18. *Ibid.*, 3–4.

19. Annette Gordon-Reed, and Peter S. Onuf, *"Most Blessed of Patriarchs": Thomas Jefferson and the Empire of the Imagination* (New York: W. Norton & Company, 2016), 79.

20. O'Shaughnessy, *supra* note 10, 19.

21. McCullough, *1776, supra* note 15, Photograph 14, with Caption.

22. Joseph Ellis, *Founding Brothers: The Revolutionary Generation* (New York: Vintage Books, 2000), 130–131.

23. Sun Tzu, *The Art of War* (Harrisburg: The Military Service Publishing Co., 1944) (reprinted by Dover in 2002), 48.

24. O'Shaughnessy, *supra* note 10, 118.

25. *Ibid.*

26. Nancy Isenberg, *Fallen Founder: The Life of Aaron Burr* (New York: Penguin Books, 2007), 42–43.

27. Benjamin Quarles, *The Negro in the American Revolution* (Williamsburg: The Omohundro Institute of Early American History and Culture, 1961, 1991), 73.

28. *Ibid.*

29. Higginbotham, *supra* note 13, 136–137.

30. *Ibid.*, 372.

31. Annette Gordon-Reed, *The Hemingses of Monticello* (New York: Norton, 2008), 135.

32. Ira Berlin, *Slaves Without Masters* (New York: The New Press, 1974), 17–18.

33. *Ibid.*, 18–19.

34. T.O. Madden Jr., *We Were Always Free: The Maddens of Culpeper Country, Virginia* (Charlottesville: University of Virginia Press, 1992), 191.

35. *Ibid.*, 43, 191–199.

36. Berlin, *supra* note 32, 19.

37. Dred Scott v. Sanford, 60 U.S. 393, 407 (1857).

38. Higginbotham, *supra* note 13, 137–138.

39. *Ibid.*, 139.

40. Nancy Isenberg, *Fallen Founder: The Life of Aaron Burr* (New York: Penguin Books, 2007), 90.

41. Higginbotham, *supra* note 13, 139.

42. June Purcell Guild, *Black Laws of Virginia* (1936) (Westminster: Heritage Books, 1995, 2011), 158.

43. Higginbotham, *supra* note 13, 372, 474–475 (citing William C. Nell, *The Colored Patriots of the American Revolution* . . . with an introduction by Harriet Beecher Stowe (New York: Arno Press and The New York Times, 1968), p. 5.).

44. Berlin, *supra* note 32, 46. (The modified version of this Table appears in *Slaves Without Masters*).

45. While Berlin list the number of Free Blacks in Virginia at 12,66 on page 46, that appears to have been a mistake, with the actual number as 12,886. *See, e.g.,* Joseph Ellis, *Founding Brothers, supra* note 22, 102.

46. Berlin, *supra* note 32, 47.

47. Solomon Northup, *12 Years a Slave* (New York: Penguin Books, 2013 (First published in the United States by Derby and Miller, 1853), 169.

48. Guild, *supra* note 42, 117.

49. *Ibid.*, 112.

50. Chapter 68 (1834) provided,

A free Negro shall not migrate into this Commonwealth from any state in the Union, or from any foreign country, under penalty of thirty-nine lashes on his bare back at the public whipping post. Returning after removal is to be punished according to the act of 1819. Special fines and penalties are set for masters of vessels who bring in any free Negroes. An exception is made for travelers who have any free Negroes in their employment.

Ibid., 109.

51. Chapter 23 (1793) provided,

This act forbids free Negroes or mulattoes from migrating into the Commonwealth. If they come in, they may be exported to the place from which they came. Every Master of a vessel or other persons who shall bring into this Commonwealth by water or by land any free Negro shall forfeit one hundred pounds, one-half of to the Commonwealth and the other half to the informer.

Ibid., 95.

52. *Ibid.*

53. *Ibid.*

54. *Ibid.*, 79.

55. *Ibid.*

56. *Ibid.*

57. *Ibid.*, 79–80.

58. *Ibid.*, 109.

59. *Ibid.*

Chapter Eight

1. John Russell, *The Free Negro in Virginia, 1619–1865* (Baltimore: The John Hopkins Press, 1913), 55–56.

2. *Ibid.*, 57.

3. *Ibid.*, 57–58.

4. *Ibid.*, 58.

5. Ron Chernow, *Alexander Hamilton* (New York: Penguin Books, 2004), 210.

6. Russell, *supra* note 1, 54–60.

7. *Ibid.*, 54–56.

8. *Ibid.*, 54–55.

9. *Ibid.*, 59.

10. *Ibid.*, 55.

11. *Ibid.*, 54–55.

12. *Ibid.*, 55–56 (quoting MS. Petitions, Hanover County, 1785; Frederick County, 1786, A6340).

13. *Ibid.*, 59.

14. June Purcell Guild, *Black Laws of Virginia* (1936) (Westminster: Heritage Books, 1995, 2011), 61.

15. *Ibid.*, 65.

16. Russell, *supra* note 1, 62.

17. *Ibid.*

Every [N]egro who fought or served as a free man in the late war was given in 1783 a legislative pledge of the utmost protection of the State in the enjoyment of the freedom he had helped to gain; and a slave who could prove any honorable service rendered by him to the American cause was freed by special act and at expense of the state.

18. *Ibid.*, 44–45.

19. *Ibid.*, 45.

20. Guild, *supra* note 14, 188.

21. Russell, *supra* note 1, 44.

22. *Ibid.*, 63.

23. *Ibid.*, 46.

24. President Thomas Jefferson freed several slaves in the codicil to his last will and testament. One of them was Burwell Colbert, one of his most trusted slaves who had served as his butler and personal servant. In 1812, Jefferson began paying an annual $20 gratuity to Burwell. Jefferson sometimes borrowed money from him. *See* Founders Online, *Thomas Jefferson to James Leitch, 15 February 1812, National Archives & Records Administration* http://founder.archives.gov/documents/Jefferson/3-04-02-0386 (last visited Oct. 12, 2015). Burwell Colbert was the grandson of Elizabeth Hemings, who was the mother of Sally Hemings, Jefferson's concubine. See Annette Gordon-Reed, *The Hemingses of Monticello* (New York: Norton, 2008), 668–669 (Hemings Family Tree).

25. Russell, *supra* note 1, 61.

26. *Ibid.*

27. Deed of Emancipation Crawley.pdf (On file with the Author).

28. *Ibid.*

29. Guild, *supra* note 14, 61.

30. Kathleen H. Hadfield and W. Cary McConnaughey, eds., *Historical Notes on Amelia County, Virginia* (Amelia County Historical Society, 1982), Appendix, 489.

31. Virginia Land Patent Maps are available in the Library of Virginia Map Room.

32. Hadfield and McConnaughey, *supra* note 30, Appendix, 494.

33. *Virginia Public Claims: Amelia County*, 26.

34. *Ibid.*

35. *Ibid.*, 26–27.

36. Andrew Jackson O'Shaughnessy, *The Men Who Lost America: British Leadership, the American Revolution and the Fate of the Empire* (New Haven: Yale University Press, 2013), 211.

37. Hadfield and McConnaughey, *supra* note 30, 32.

38. O'Shaughnessy, *supra* note 36, 275–276.

39. Hadfield and McConnaughey, *supra* note 30, 32.

40. *Ibid.*, 58.

41. Last Will & Testament of Benjamin Crawley (May 17, 1793) (On file with the Author).

42. *Ibid.*

43. Amelia County Deed Book 19, page 212 (1792).

44. *Ibid.*

45. *Ibid.*, 249 and 272.

46. Deed on file with the author.

47. 1810 United States Federal Census, Amelia County, Virginia; p. 244, *Familysearch.org.*

48. United States Federal Census (1810).

49. Amelia County Order Book 21, page 50.

50. Amelia County Order Book 22, page 67.

51. *Ibid.*

52. Annette Gordon-Reed, *Thomas Jefferson and Sally Hemings: An American Controversy* (Charlottesville: University of Virginia Press, 1997), 247.

53. See Lucia Stanton, *"Those Who Labor for My Happiness": Slavery at Jefferson's Monticello* (Charlottesville: University of Virginia Press, 2012), 177.

54. Sally Hemings has been featured in numerous non-fiction books, and became the main character in at least one work of fiction, namely Barbara Chase-Riboud's book called *Sally Hemings* (1979). Some of the non-fiction works include Annette Gordon-Reed's *Thomas Jefferson & Sally Hemings: An American Controversy*, (Charlottesville: University of Virginia Press, 1997), and *The Hemingses of Monticello: An American Family*. The latter won the National Book Award and a Pulitzer Prize. An entire section, with multiple chapters, is devoted to Sally Hemings in Virginia Scharff's book *The Women Jefferson Loved* 157–236 (2010). The story of Sally Hem-

ing's relationship with Thomas Jefferson is featured in Fawn Brodie's book *Thomas Jefferson: An Intimate History* 228–245 (1974).

55. Gordon-Reed, *supra* note 52, 59–77.

56. Guild, *supra* note 14, 30–31 (quoting Chapter 72).

57. *Ibid.*, 30.

58. *Ibid.*

59. *Ibid.*, 29 ("Every person of whose grandfathers or grandmothers anyone is or shall have been a Negro, although all his other progenitors, except that descending from the Negro shall have been white persons, shall be deemed a mulatto, and so every person who shall have one-fourth or more Negro blood shall in like manner be deemed a mulatto.").

60. Consider *Plessy v. Ferguson*, 163 U.S. 537 (1896) (demonstrating that this presumption changed over time. In June 1892, Homer Plessy who was one-eighth Negro was jailed for sitting in the white section of the train in New Orleans. The U.S. Supreme Court proclaimed the "separate but equal" doctrine when it upheld Louisiana's "Separate Car Act.").

61. Stanton, *supra* note 53, 8.

62. *Ibid.*, 177.

63. Annette Gordon-Reed and Peter S. Onuf, *"Most Blessed of Patriarchs": Thomas Jefferson and the Empire of the Imagination* (New York: W. Norton & Company, 2016), 23.

64. Gordon Reed, *supra* note 52, 246.

65. *Ibid.*

66. See Last Will and Testament of Thomas Jefferson, available at http://www.monticello.org/site/research-and-collections/last-will-and-testament, for information about Jefferson's freeing Sally Hemings' relatives through the codicil to his will.

67. Gordon-Reed, *supra* note 52, 246.

68. *Ibid.*, 248.

69. See *Catalogue of the Officers and Students in Yale College, 1843–4* (New Haven: B.L. Hamlen, 1843), 22. *See also, The History of Linn County, Missouri: An Encyclopedia of Useful Information, and a Compendium of Actual Facts* (Kansas City: Birdsall & Dean, 1882), 762.

70. Guild, *supra* note 14, 32.

71. *Ibid.*

Chapter Nine

1. F. Scott Fitzgerald, "F. Scott Fitzgerald Quotes," *Famous Quotes at BrainyQuote*.http://www.brainyquote.com/quotes/quotes/f/fscottfit100572.html#sDcgtR9yu3rd4Euc.99

2. John B. Boles, *Jefferson: Architect of American Liberty* (New York: Basic Books, 2017), 177–178.

3. Lucia Stanton, "*Those Who Labor for My Happiness*": Slavery at Jefferson's Monticello (Charlottesville: University of Virginia Press, 2012), 3.

4. June Purcell Guild, *Black Laws of Virginia* (1936) (Westminster: Heritage Books, 1995, 2011), 167, 179.

5. Stanton, *supra* note 3, 22–23.

6. *Ibid.*, 22.

7. https://en.wikipedia.org/wiki/Doublethink

8. Stanton, *supra* note 3, 19.

9. Edward Baptist, *And The Half Has Never Been Told* (New York: Basic Books, 2014), 116–117.

10. https://en.wikipedia.org/wiki/Cognitive_dissonance

11. Boles, *supra* note 2, 177.

12. Annette Gordon-Reed, *Thomas Jefferson and Sally Hemings: An American Controversy* (Charlottesville: University of Virginia Press, 1997), 254.

13. Stanton, *supra* note 3, 177.

14. See Annette Gordon-Reed, *The Hemingses of Monticello* (New York: Norton, 2008), 669–67 (showcasing the family tree of Sally Hemings. In the family tree, Sally's parents were Betsy Hemings, a half-African, half-English slave and her father was John Wayles.).

15. Madison Hemings, a son who resulted from this union, gave an interview to a radical Republican newspaper editor in 1873 in which he retold the story of how his mother became Mr. Jefferson's concubine while the two were in France. Scharff, Virginia, *The Women Jefferson Loved* (New York: Harper Perennial 2010), 214–15. He said he had lost contact with Beverly and Harriet who both passed as whites and married whites in "good circumstances" or in "good standing." Gordon-Reed, *supra* note 12, 246.

16. In 1815, in a letter correcting an erroneous statement of law that he had made to a man who had asked when a black person could be con-

sidered a white person under the laws of Virginia, Jefferson wrote out an algebraic equation demonstrating that after "three crossings" with whites, the black person was legally white.

Gordon-Reed, supra note 12, 53.

17. *See* Stanton, *supra* note 3.

18. H.W. Brands, *The First American: The Life and Times of Benjamin Franklin* (New York: Anchor Books, 2000), 15.

19. *Ibid.*, 21–22.

20. Benjamin Franklin, *The Autobiography of Benjamin Franklin* (Mineola, Dover Publications, Inc., 1996), 15.

21. Brands, *supra* note 19, 33–34.

22. Walter Isaacson, *Benjamin Franklin: An American Life* (New York: Simon & Schuster, 2003), 151–152.

23. *Ibid.*, 152.

24. David McCullough, *John Adams* (New York: Simon & Schuster, 2001), 132.

25. Isaascson, *supra* note 22, 151.

26. *Ibid.*, 702.

27. *Ibid.*, 703.

28. *Ibid.*, 704.

29. *Ibid.*

30. The website dedicated to Franklin's life wrote,

Benjamin Franklin was a slaveholder for most of his life. The enslaved Africans who are mentioned in Franklin's correspondence include Peter, Jemima, Othello (who died young), King, and George. While he wrote in his 1757 will 'that my Negro Man Peter, and his Wife Jemima, be free after my Decease,' they died before Franklin, who did not own any slaves at the end of his life. In his later years Franklin became an ardent abolitionist, and in his final will Franklin stipulated that his son-in-law, Richard Bache, should not receive his inheritance unless he freed his slave, Bob.

"Benjamin Franklin and Slavery," in the section *The Benjamin Franklin Tercentenary*, http://www.benfranklin300.org/exhibition/_html/2_2/index.htm (last visited Oct. 12, 2015). According to another publication from this organization, Franklin spent his last years, in part, promoting the abolishment of slavery. "Benjamin Franklin: In Search of a Better World," *The*

Benjamin Franklin Tercentenary, http://www.ala.org/ programming/sites/ ala.org.programming/files/content/franklin/materials/Benjamin_Franklin_Br1.pdf (last visited Oct. 12, 2015).

31. Sherri Burr, "Max as Mentor" in *Max Evans & A Few Friends: The 90th Birthday Book*, ed. Ollie Reed Jr., Slim Randles & Ruth E. Francis (Los Ranchos: Rio Grande Books, 2014), 84. Author Max Evans wrote a memoir about film director Sam Peckinpah, "whom he considers to be among 'the immortals,' those who contribute to humanity in such a manner as to guarantee they will be remembered for decades, if not centuries, after their passing to the Great Mystery in the Sky." This phrase seemed an apt reference for Benjamin Franklin as well.

32. Nancy Isenberg, *Fallen Founder: The Life of Aaron Burr* (New York: Penguin Books, 2007), 91. Ron Chernow, *Alexander Hamilton* (New York: Penguin Books, 2004), 214–216.

33. Isenberg, *ibid.*, 90.

34. *Ibid.*

35. Gordon-Reed, *The Hemingses of Monticello, supra* note 14, 99–100.

36. Isenberg, *Fallen Founder, supra* note 32, 91.

37. *Ibid.*

38. Stanton, *supra* note 3, 23.

39. Isenberg, *supra* note 32, 153.

40. Author Sherri Burr is working on a book tentatively named *Aaron Burr's Family of Color: A Legacy of Love, Public Service, and the Underground Railroad*.

41. Oliver Perry Sturm, *The Conspiracy Against Aaron Burr* (1943) (Edited by the Aaron Burr Association, 2005), 257.

42. Letter dated September 30, 2004, from Luella Burr Mitchell Allen to Henry Anderson of the Aaron Burr Association. The letter states that "John Pierre, listed as John Burr, passenger-born-at-sea Aug. 26, 1792. Also passenger listed would be John's mother, Mary Burr." (On file with the Author)

43. Sturm, *supra* note 41, 257.

44. *Ibid.*, 256.

45. F.J. Webb, *The Garies and Their Friends* (New York: Routlede & Co., 1857), v.

46. Records for the 5 Pennsylvania Regiment (Revolutionary War), p. 543 (1777) (On file with the Author).

47. Allen B. Ballard, *One More Day's Journey: The Story of a Family and a People* (Lincoln: An Authors Guild Backinprint.Com Edition published by iUniverse.com, 2004), 5.

48. *Ibid.*, 68–69.

49. *Ibid.*, 69.

50. Cornish, Mabel Burr, "Anti-Slavery Movements: Authentic" (Philadelphia, PA, 1935). This letter was given to Miriam Burr Mitchell Cooper, a great-great granddaughter of John Pierre Burr, and is on file with the Author.

51. John Chester Miller, *The Wolf by the Ears: Thomas Jefferson and Slavery* (Charlottesville: The University Press of Virginia, 1991), 22.

52. Boles, *supra* note 2, 403.

53. See Peter Charles Hoffer, *The Treason Trials of Aaron Burr* (Lawrence: University Press of Kansas, 2008).

54. Chernow, *Alexander Hamilton*, *supra* note 32, 210.

55. *Ibid.*, 211.

56. Boles, *supra* note 2, 461.

57. Chernow, *Alexander Hamilton*, *supra* note 32, 210.

58. *Ibid.*

59. Frank Monaghan, *John Jay, Defender of Liberty* (New York: The Bobbs-Merrill Company, 1935).

60. Gordon-Reed, *The Hemingses of Monticello, supra* note 14, 178–179.

61. *Ibid.*, 179.

62. Walter Stahr, *John Jay: Founding Father* (London: Hambledon and London, 2005), 190.

63. Gordon-Reed, *The Hemingses of Monticello, supra* note 14, 179.

64. *Ibid.*, 179.

65. Stahr, *supra* note 62, 193.

66. David McCullough, *1776* (New York: Simon & Schuster, 2005), 227.

67. *Ibid.*

68. Joseph Ellis, *His Excellency George Washington* (New York: Alfred A. Knopf, 2004), 45.

69. "George Washington & Slavery," *available at* https://www.mount vernon.org/george-washington/slavery/?gclid=EAIaIQobChMIv_WZiaLY 4AIVQx-tBh0PNwNlEAAYASAAEgKWk_D_BwE.

70. Ellis, *supra* note 68, 46.

71. Erica Armstrong Dunbar, *Never Caught: the Washingtons' relentless pursuit of their runaway slave, Ona Judge* (New York: Atria Books, 2017).

72. Boles, *supra* note 2, 415.

73. *Ibid.*, 463.

74. Annette Gordon-Reed and Peter Onuf, *"Most Blessed of Patriarchs": Thomas Jefferson and the Empire of the Imagination*, (New York: W. Norton & Company, 2016), 55.

75. Gordon-Reed, *The Hemingses of Monticello, supra* note 14, 444.

76. *Ibid.*

77. Benjamin Quarles, *The Negro in the American Revolution* (Williamsburg: The Omohundro Institute of Early American History and Culture, 1961, 1991) 187.

78. *Ibid.*

79. "George Washington & Slavery," *supra* note 69.

80. McCullough, *supra* note 66, 90.

81. "George Washington & Slavery," *supra* note 69.

82. Boles, *supra* note 2, 228–230.

83. Gordon-Reed, *The Hemingses of Monticello, supra* note 14, 475–476.

84. Boles, *supra* note 2, 177–178.

85. Gordon-Reed, *The Hemingses of Monticello, supra* note 14, 97.

86. Boles, *supra* note 2, 45.

87. Gordon-Reed, *The Hemingses of Monticello, supra* note 14, 631.

88. Boles, *supra* note 2, 512.

89. Stanton, *supra* note 3, 4.

90. Ellis, *supra* note 68, 45.

91. See "Ten Facts about Washington and Slavery," available at https://www.mountvernon.org/george-washington/slavery/ten-facts-about-washington-slavery/ (last visited on February 25, 2019).

92. See Last Will and Testament of Thomas Jefferson, available at http://www.monticello.org/site/research-and-collections/last-will-and-testament, for information about Jefferson's freeing Sally Hemings' relatives through the codicil to his will.

93. The United States Constitution, Article 1, Section 2, Clause 3.

94. Letter from James Madison to Frances Wright, 1 September 1825. Accessed February 25, 2019, https://founders.archives.gov/documents/Madison/04-03-02-0612.

95. Quote available at https://en.wikiquote.org/wiki/James_Monroe. Accessed February 25, 2019,

96. Gordon-Reed, *The Hemingses of Monticello, supra* note 14, 653.

97. *Ibid.,* 654.

98. Boles, *supra* note 2, 230.

Chapter Ten

1. John Russell, *The Free Negro in Virginia, 1619–1865* (Baltimore: The John Hopkins Press, 1913), 13.

2. *Ibid.,* 9.

3. Luther Porter Jackson, *Free Negro Labor and Property Holding in Virginia, 1830–1860* (New York: Athenum, 1969), ix–x.

4. 1840 Census.pdf (On file with the Author).

5. *Ibid.*

6. Russell, *supra* note 1, 64–65.

7. *Ibid.,* 51.

8. David S. Reynolds, *John Brown, Abolitionist: The Man Who Killed Slavery, Sparked the Civil War, and Seeded Civil Rights* (New York: Alfred A. Knopf, 2005), 52.

9. *Ibid.,* 108–109.

10. June Purcell Guild, *Black Laws of Virginia* (1936) (Westminster: Heritage Books, 1995, 2011), 72.

Slaves brought into this state and kept one year shall be forfeited by the owner, and the right to the slaves shall rest in the overseers of the poor, who shall apprehend such slaves for the benefit of the poor. If any slave hereafter emancipated shall remain within this Commonwealth more than twelve months after his freedom, he shall forfeit such right, and may be sold by the overseers for the benefit of the poor.

11. *Ibid.,* 117.

12. See generally, Ted Maris-Wolf, *Family Bonds: Free Blacks and Reenslavement Law in Antebellum Virginia* (Chapel Hill: The University of North Carolina Press, 2015).

13. See Ellen D. Katz, "African-American Freedom in Antebellum Cumberland County, Virginia, 70 *Chi.-Kent L. Rev.* 1995), 927, 961–62 (1995).

14. Russell, *supra* note 1, 72.

15. A. Leon Higginbotham, *In the Matter of Color: Race and the American Legal Process, The Colonial Period* (New York: Oxford University Press, 1978), 207 ("The legislature displayed its fear of the rising black population, whether slave or free, in another 1800 act that prohibited the entry into South Carolina of any free Negro or any 'slave of servant or color, [brought in] for sale within this state. . . .' Free blacks entering or brought into South Carolina in violation of this act were ordered to be sold after the violation was established by jury verdict.").

16. Joan W. Peters, *Introduction* to June Purcell Guild, *Black Laws of Virginia* (Westminster: Heritage Books, 2011, 1936), at [pincite to first page of introduction] (1995).

17. *Ibid.*

18. *Ibid.*

19. Free Black Register Dinwiddie Co VA.pdf (On file with the Author).

20. *Ibid.*

21. *Ibid.*

22. Julia Hill Marriage.pdf (On file with the Author).

23. Guild, *supra* note 10, 95.

24. Davenport v. Commonwealth, 28 Va. 588, 592–593 (1829).

25. *Ibid.*, 593.

26. *Ibid.*

27. 1860 U.S. census, Virginia, Petersburg City, South Ward, page no. 35, dwelling no. 333, family no. 333, Sarah Hill; Familysearch.org, last accessed June 15, 2018, https://www.familysearch.org/ark:/61903/3:1:33SQ-GBSF-9RTK?i=34&cc=1473181 (Free with account creation)] .

28. 1870 U.S. census, Virginia, Petersburg City, 5th Ward, page 51, dwelling 421, family no. 452, Celia Hill; Familysearch.org, last accessed June 15, 2018, https://www.familysearch.org/ark:/61903/3:1:S3HT-6L9G-7H?i=50&cc=1438024 (Free with account creation)].

29. 1810 U.S. census, Virginia, Dinwiddie County, Petersburg, page no. 118, William Prentis; Familysearch.org, last accessed June 14, 2018, https://www.familysearch.org/ark:/61903/3:1:33SQ-GYBZ-W1R (Free with account creation).

30. Luther Porter Jackson, *Rights and Duties in A Democracy* (August 14, 1946) (Available in the Special Collections/Archives in Virginia State University's Johnston Memorial Library).

31. Russell, *supra* note 1, 125.

32. Katz, *supra* note 13, 961.

33. Research would later reveal that Daniel Hardaway, who apprenticed Gideon Hill, was a seventh cousin of Cheryl Burbank, who is Sherri Burr's University of New Mexico assistant and helped with the census research for this book. On a July 22, 1802, tax record, Gideon appeared on a list of Free Negroes living on the property of Daniel Hardaway as a blacksmith. Since he was about 17 at the time, he most likely was an apprentice blacksmith.

34. Document on file with the author.

35. Letter documenting Gideon Hill's Purchase of Property (On file with the Author).

36. Jackson, *supra* note 30.

37. Katz, *supra* note 13, 930–931 (citing John H. Franklin, "Free Negro in the Economic Life of Ante-bellum North Carolina (pt. 1)," 19 *N.C. Hist. Rev.* 239, 366–67 (1942).

38. Katz, *ibid.*, 928.

39. *Ibid.*

40. Luther Porter Jackson, *Free Negro Labor and Property Holding in Virginia, 1830–1860* (New York: Atheneum, 1969), App. I, at 241.

41. *Ibid.*

42. Russell, *supra* note 1, 13 ("In the mountainous half of the State, which after 1830 contained half of the white population, free [N]egroes were so scarce as to be an almost negligible social factor . . . . Of the 12,866 free [N]egroes in Virginia in 1790 only 75 resided in Trans-Alleghany, or what is now West Virginia").

43. *Ibid.*, 14.

44. Document on file with the author.

45. Jackson, *supra* note 40, Appendix I, 241.

46. *Ibid.*

47. *Ibid.*, Appendix I, 244.

48. Russell, *supra* note 1, 125.

49. 1850 Census.pdf (On file with the Author).

50. Joshua Rothman, Notorious *in the Neighborhood: Sex and Families Across the Color Line in Virginia, 1787–1861* (Chapel Hill: The University of North Carolina Press, 2003), 169–198.

51. *Ibid.*, 174.

52. *Ibid.*, 178.

53. *Ibid.*, 169–170.

54. *Ibid.*, 187.

55. *Ibid.*, 190–191.

56. Guild, *supra* note 10, 31.

57. Rothman, *supra* note 50, 174.

58. *Ibid.*, 180.

59. Guild, *supra* note 10, 32.

60. *Ibid.*

61. Rothman, *supra* note 50, 178.

62. *Ibid.*, 179.

63. *Ibid.*, 178–179.

64. *Ibid.*, 193–194.

65. Suzanne Lebsock, *The Free Women of Petersburg, Status and Culture in a Southern Town, 1784–1860* (New York: W.W. Norton & Company, 1984), 235–236.

66. *Ibid.*

67. Russell, *supra* note 1, 153.

68. *Ibid.*

69. *Ibid.*, 153–154.

70. *Ibid.*, 154.

71. *Ibid.*

72. Jackson, *supra* note 40.

73. Russell, *supra* note 1, 151.

74. Katz, *supra* note 13, 933.

75. Ira Berlin, *Foreword* to Heinegg, Paul, *Free African Americans of North Carolina, Virginia, and South Carolina: From the Colonial Period to About 1820* , 5th Ed. (Baltimore: Clearfield Company, 2005), v, vi.

76. Katz, *supra* note 13, 974–975.

77. *Ibid.*, 975.

78. *Ibid.*

79. *Ibid.*, 975 n.312.

80. *Ibid.*

81. Guild, *supra* note 10, 96 (reproducing Chapter LVIII from 1810).

82. *Ibid.*

83. *Ibid.*

84. Russell, *supra* note 1, 133.

85. Katz, *supra* note 13, 961–62.

86. Guild, *supra* note 10, 96 (reproducing Chapter LXXVIII from 1810).

87. Guild, *supra* note 10, 97 (reproducing Chapter LXXIX–LXXX from 1811).

88. *Ibid.*, 97 (reproducing Chapter CXXVIII from 1812).

89. *Ibid.*, 112.

90. *Ibid.,* 117.

91. A. Leon Higginbotham, and Greer C. Bosworth, "'Rather Than the Free': Free Blacks in Colonial and Antebellum Virginia," 26 *Harv. C.R.-Civ. Liberties L. Rev.* 17, 25–33 (1991).

92. *Ibid.*

93. Christa Dierksheide, *Amelioration and Empire: Progress and Slavery in the Plantation Americas* (Charlottesville: The University of Virginia Press, 2014), 137.

94. *Ibid.*

95. Ira Berlin, *Slaves Without Masters* (New York: The New Press, 1974).

96. Solomon Northup, *Twelve Years a Slave* (New York: Penguin Books, 2013).

97. Kirt Von Daacke, *Freedom has a Face: Race, Identity, and Community in Jefferson's Virginia* (Charlottesville: University of Virginia Press, 2012), 1.

98. *Ibid.*, 4.

99. *Ibid.*

100. *Ibid.*, 5.

101. Berlin, *supra* note 95, xiii.

102. *Ibid.*

Chapter Eleven

1. John Russell, *The Free Negro in Virginia, 1619–1865* (Baltimore: The John Hopkins Press, 1913), 15.

2. *Ibid.*

3. *Ibid.*

4. John Chester Miller, *The Wolf by the Ears: Thomas Jefferson and Slavery* (Charlottesville: The University Press of Virginia, 1991), 241.

5. *Ibid.*

6. Zora Neale Hurston, *Barracoon: the Story of the Last "Black Cargo"* (New York: Amistad, 2018).

7. Edward Baptist, *And The Half Has Never Been Told* (New York: Basic Books, 2014), 246.

8. *Ibid.*, 244.

9. Miller, *supra* note 4, 41.

10. Annette Gordon-Reed, *The Hemingses of Monticello* (New York: Norton, 2008), 320–323.

11. *Ibid.*, 321.

12. Ron Chernow, *Grant* (New York: Penguin Press, 2017), 505.

13. Adam Serwer, "The Myth of the Kindly General Lee: The legend of the Confederate leader's heroism and decency is based in the fiction of a person who never existed," *The Atlantic* (June 4, 2017).

14. Booker T. Washington, *Up from Slavery* (New York: Penguin Books, 1901, 1986), 17.

15. *Ibid.*, 17–18.

16. *Ibid.*, 21.

17. Serwer, *supra* note 13.

18. *Ibid.*

19. *Ibid.*

20. *Glory*, Directed by Edward Zwick (1989).

21. Serwer, *supra* note 13.

22. Annette Gordon-Reed and Peter S. Onuf, *"Most Blessed of Patriarchs": Thomas Jefferson and the Empire of the Imagination* (New York: W. Norton & Company, 2016), 16.

23. Allen B. Ballard, *One More Day's Journey: The Story of a Family and a People* (Lincoln: An Authors Guild Backinprint.com Edition published by iUniverse.com, 2004), 6.

24. Russell, *supra* note 1, 14–15.

25. Chernow, *supra* note 12, 410–411.

26. Ulysses S. Grant, *Personal Memoirs of U.S. Grant* (Cambridge: Da Capo Press, 2001), 454.

27. *Ibid.*, 538.

28. Elizabeth Keckley, *Behind the Scenes. Or, Thirty Years a Slave, and Four Years in the White House* (New York: Oxford University Press, 1988), 162.

29. *Ibid.*, 17.

30. *Ibid.*, 35, 39.

31. *Ibid.*, 169.

32. *Ibid.*, 74–75.

33. David Brion Davis, *The Problem of Slavery in the Age of Emancipation* (2014), 193 (quoting Frederick Douglas).

34. Albert L. Johnson Jr., *Minute Book Genealogy of Williamson County, Tennessee (1799–1865)*, 129 (document on file with the author).

35. *Ibid.*

36. Eric Foner, *Why Reconstruction Matters*, N.Y. Times, Mar. 28, 2015, http://www.nytimes.com/2015/03/29/opinion/sunday/why-reconstruction -matters.html?_r=0 (explaining that "[r]econstruction refers to the period, generally dated from 1865 to 1877, during which the nation's laws and Constitution were rewritten to guarantee the basic rights of the former slaves, and biracial governments came to power throughout the defeated Confederacy").

37. June Purcell Guild, *Black Laws of Virginia* (1936) (Westminster: Heritage Books, 1995, 2011), 33.

38. Jones v. Commonwealth, 80 Va. 538 (Va. 1885).

39. *Ibid.*, 541–542 (Va. 1885).

40. *Ibid.*, 544–545 (Va. 1885).

41. Guild, *supra* note 37, 35 ("Every person having one-sixteenth or more Negro blood shall be deemed a colored person, and every person not a colored person having one-fourth or more of Indian blood shall be deemed an Indian.").

42. No marriage license shall be granted unless the clerk has reasonable assurance that the statements as to color are correct. It shall be unlawful for any white person to marry any save a white person, or a person with no other admixture of blood than white and American Indian. The term "white person" shall apply only to the person who has no trace whatsoever of any blood other than Caucasian, but persons who have one-sixteenth or less of the blood of the American Indian, and no other non-Caucasic [*sic*] blood shall be deemed white persons.
Guild, *ibid.*, 35.

Horrigon contends that this act was the beginning of the one-drop rule in Virginia, and that the time frame overlapped with the eugenics research that claimed to prove the inferiority of black and native people. Horrigan, Meghan Carr, *The State of Marriage in Virginia History: A Legislative Means of Identifying the Cultural Other*, 9 Geo. J. Gender & L. 379, 389 (2008). An irony is that they considered Black blood to be genetically dominant and thus one drop could contaminate and corrupt an otherwise white race. *Ibid.*

43. Guild, *supra* note 37, 35–36.

44. John Punch → John Bunch I → John Bunch II → John Bunch III → Samuel Bunch → Charles Bunch → Nathanial Bunch → Anna Bunch → Frances Allred → Margaret Wright → Leona McCurry → Madelyn Payne → Stanley Ann Dunham → Barack Obama. Many thanks to Brandon Ilgen, a descendant of John Punch and a member of the University of New Mexico Law School Class of 2019, for giving me this family tree on November 15, 2018. The tree remains on file with the author.

Epilogue

1. Part of this epilogue has been delivered in speeches and was published in the newsletter called *Legacy: New Mexico Jewish Historical Society* (Winter 2017–2018). After Dianne Layden heard me speak to launch the "Lawyers without Rights" exhibition at the University of New Mexico School of Law in February 2017, she asked me write up a version of my speech for the *Legacy* Newsletter. Linney Wix, Ph.D., was the secretary of the New Mexico Holocaust Museum Board of Directors when she requested the University of New Mexico Law School host the exhibition.

2. See David Cesarani, *Final Solution: The Fate of the Jews 1933–1949* (New York: St. Martin's Press, 2016).

3. James Q. Whitman, *Hitler's American Model: The United States and the Making of Nazi Race Law* (Princeton: Princeton University Press, 2017), 1–2.

4. *Ibid.*, 2.

5. *Ibid.*, 3.

6. Trevor Noah, *Born a Crime* (New York: Penguin, Random House, 2016), i.

7. *Ibid.*

8. *Ibid.*

9. The Truth and Reconciliation Commission of South Africa, Volume One, Chapter 2, presented to President Nelson Mandela on 29 October 1998, 30.

10. *Ibid.*, 31.

11. Adam Serwer, "The Myth of the Kindly General Lee: The legend of the Confederate leader's heroism and decency is based in the fiction of a person who never existed," *The Atlantic* (June 4, 2017) (quoting historian Eric Foner's book *Reconstruction*).

Index